The Joy of Hearing

New Testament Theology

Edited by Thomas R. Schreiner and Brian S. Rosner

The Mission of the Triune God: A Theology of Acts, Patrick Schreiner

The Joy of Hearing: A Theology of the Book of Revelation, Thomas R. Schreiner

The Joy of Hearing

A Theology of the Book of Revelation

Thomas R. Schreiner

CROSSWAY®

WHEATON, ILLINOIS

The Joy of Hearing: A Theology of the Book of Revelation
Copyright © 2021 by Thomas R. Schreiner
Published by Crossway
   1300 Crescent Street
   Wheaton, Illinois 60187

Cover design: Kevin Lipp
First printing 2021
Printed in the United States of America

Trade paperback ISBN: 978-1-4335-7132-9
ePub ISBN: 978-1-4335-7135-0
PDF ISBN: 978-1-4335-7133-6
Mobipocket ISBN: 978-1-4335-7134-3

Library of Congress Cataloging-in-Publication Data

Names: Schreiner, Thomas R., author.
Title: The joy of hearing : a theology of the book of Revelation / Thomas R. Schreiner.
Description: Wheaton, Illinois : Crossway, 2021. | Series: New Testament theology | Includes bibliographical references and index.
Identifiers: LCCN 2020046763 (print) | LCCN 2020046764 (ebook) | ISBN 9781433571329 (trade paperback) | ISBN 9781433571336 (pdf) | ISBN 9781433571343 (mobipocket) | ISBN 9781433571350 (epub)
Subjects: LCSH: Bible. Revelation—Theology.
Classification: LCC BS2825.52 .S45 2021 (print) | LCC BS2825.52 (ebook) | DDC 228/.06—dc23
LC record available at https://lccn.loc.gov/2020046763
LC ebook record available at https://lccn.loc.gov/2020046764

Crossway is a publishing ministry of Good News Publishers.

VP		30	29	28	27	26	25	24	23	22	21
15	14	13	12	11	10	9	8	7	6	5	4	3	2	1

Contents

Tables

Series Preface

THERE ARE REMARKABLY FEW treatments of the big ideas of single books of the New Testament. Readers can find brief coverage in Bible dictionaries, in some commentaries, and in New Testament theologies, but such books are filled with other information and are not devoted to unpacking the theology of each New Testament book in its own right. Technical works concentrating on various themes of New Testament theology often have a narrow focus, treating some aspect of the teaching of, say, Matthew or Hebrews in isolation from the rest of the book's theology.

The New Testament Theology series seeks to fill this gap by providing students of Scripture with readable book-length treatments of the distinctive teaching of each New Testament book or collection of books. The volumes approach the text from the perspective of biblical theology. They pay due attention to the historical and literary dimensions of the text, but their main focus is on presenting the teaching of particular New Testament books about God and his relations to the world on their own terms, maintaining sight of the Bible's overarching narrative and Christocentric focus. Such biblical theology is of fundamental importance to biblical and expository preaching and informs exegesis, systematic theology, and Christian ethics.

The twenty volumes in the series supply comprehensive, scholarly, and accessible treatments of theological themes from an evangelical perspective. We envision them being of value to students, preachers, and interested laypeople. When preparing an expository sermon series, for example, pastors can find a healthy supply of informative commentaries, but there are few options for coming to terms with the overall teaching of each book of the New Testament. As well as being useful in sermon and Bible study preparation, the volumes will also be of value as textbooks in college and seminary exegesis classes. Our prayer is that they contribute to a deeper understanding of and commitment to the kingdom and glory of God in Christ.

Tom Schreiner's Revelation volume, *The Joy of Hearing*, takes on the urgent task of explaining the teaching of the most puzzling book in the New Testament. The book of Revelation throws up formidable interpretive challenges, not least in terms of determining its historical setting and understanding its apocalyptic imagery. Schreiner's work aims to enable readers to experience the climax of biblical prophecy in all its fullness. In our day of relentless outrage and bitter conflict, Revelation offers a powerful message of comfort, encouragement, and hope. It discloses our world's true state of affairs and offers a glimpse of transcendent reality. According to Schreiner, the joy of hearing Revelation consists of heeding the call of Jesus, listening to the words of the Spirit, and remaining confident that God rules on his throne.

Thomas R. Schreiner and Brian S. Rosner

Preface

I DECIDED TO WRITE THIS short book on the theology of the book of Revelation when I was invited to give the Moore College Lectures in August 2020. I am currently writing the Baker Exegetical Commentary on Revelation, and I have also written a shorter commentary on the book in the ESV Expository Commentary published by Crossway (2018). I tried out some of the material for this book at the Northeast Regional Meeting of the Evangelical Theological Society held at Gordon-Conwell Theological Seminary in 2019, and I am grateful for the feedback I received there and for the wonderful generosity of Eckhard and Barbara Schnabel, who hosted me in their home during those days. I also gave these lectures at Gateway Seminary in Ontario, California, in August 2019, and I learned much from the interaction and responses of those present on that occasion as well. I particularly enjoyed spending time with and getting to know John Taylor, who invited me to Gateway.

In the providence of God, I didn't give the lectures at Moore College after all. COVID-19 intervened, and thus my trip was canceled. I was at Moore College on an earlier occasion, and I was disappointed that I could not be present with them again. Still, the book of Revelation reminds us that we live in a sinful world and that God rules over all that happens. When we think of the devastating effects of the coronavirus worldwide, the disappointment of not giving the lectures at Moore College is a minor annoyance. In any case, what a joy it has been to reflect on the theology of the book of Revelation with its stunning vision of God's majesty and glory, the beautiful portrait of Jesus as the Lion and the Lamb, and the assurance that comes from knowing that the Spirit utters the word of God. Our opponents are implacable and full of hate, but our God is greater still. We are called to endurance and must refuse compromise, for God will judge those who give themselves to evil, and he promises to reward those who continue to trust him with the greatest joy of all: we shall see his face (Rev. 22:4).

I am grateful to one of my doctoral students, Coye Still IV, who checked references for me and sent me articles I requested. He saved me much time by carrying out such tasks! Also, I am so thankful to Justin Taylor and Dane Ortlund at Crossway. I had no idea what they would think of the book, but they were eager to publish it, which was very encouraging. They then suggested a series of similar books on every book of the New Testament, and Brian Rosner and I are honored to serve as editors of this series. Finally, I am grateful to David Barshinger for his fine editing and helpful suggestions, which made the book better than it would otherwise have been.

Thomas R. Schreiner
April 1, 2020

Abbreviations

AB	Anchor Bible
ACT	Ancient Christian Texts
BBR	*Bulletin for Biblical Research*
BECNT	Baker Exegetical Commentary on the New Testament
EvQ	*Evangelical Quarterly*
HNTC	Harper's New Testament Commentaries
HSM	Harvard Semitic Monographs
JBL	*Journal of Biblical Literature*
JETS	*Journal of the Evangelical Theological Society*
JSNTSup	Journal for the Study of the New Testament Supplement Series
LCL	Loeb Classical Library
NCB	New Century Bible
NICNT	New International Commentary on the New Testament
NICOT	New International Commentary on the Old Testament
NIGTC	New International Greek Testament Commentary
NovT	*Novum Testamentum*
NSBT	New Studies in Biblical Theology
OTL	Old Testament Library
PCNT	Paideia Commentaries on the New Testament
PTMS	Princeton Theological Monograph Series
SBLDS	Society of Biblical Literature Dissertation Series
SBT	Studies in Biblical Theology

Sib. Or.	Sibylline Oracles
SOTBT	Studies in Old Testament Biblical Theology
VCSup	Supplements to Vigiliae Christianae
WBC	Word Biblical Commentary
WTJ	*Westminster Theological Journal*
WUNT	Wissenschaftliche Untersuchungen zum Neuen Testament

Introduction

The Truth Apocalyptically Revealed

THE BOOK OF REVELATION both attracts and repels readers. It attracts readers because it introduces a strange new world, an apocalyptic vision that captures our imagination. We all sense that some dimensions of life are beyond us, that there are mysteries surpassing our comprehension, and Revelation introduces us to this world, inviting us to hear what God says to us. We wonder, what will happen in the future, and how will the world come to an end? Revelation reveals to us where the world is going, and it tells us what we should do to be part of the new world that is coming. At the same time, Revelation can repel us because we wonder what it all means and perhaps because we despair of making any sense of it at all. Martin Luther felt this way when he complained that Christ is not clearly taught or revealed in the book![1] Our inability to grasp the book is illustrated by this humorous comment by G. K. Chesterton: "And though St. John the Evangelist saw many strange monsters in his vision, he saw no creature so wild as one of his own commentators."[2] Perhaps we have been put off from the book when we have encountered speculative and strange readings of it, some of which offer an amazingly detailed map of what will supposedly happen in the future.

---

1   Cited in Werner Georg Kümmel, *The New Testament: The History of the Investigation of Its Problems*, trans. S. McLean Gilmour and Howard C. Kee (Nashville: Abingdon, 1972), 26.
2   G. K. Chesterton, *Orthodoxy* (New York: John Lane, 1909), 29.

My contention is that we desperately need the message of Revelation for today's world. There is a great conflict between good and evil in our world, and the Christian faith is under attack, as it was in the first century. John reminds us in this book that God rules, even in an evil day; that God has not forsaken his people; and that goodness will finally triumph and prevail. In the midst of evil, in a world in which the Christian faith is under attack, we need hope and assurance that evil will not have the last word, and Revelation teaches us that a new world is coming, that a new creation is coming, and that all will be well. God is just and holy and righteous, and those who turn against God and his Christ will suffer judgment. At the same time, we see in the book that the death and resurrection of Jesus Christ are the center of history, or the fulcrum of history. Evil has been defeated because of what Christ has accomplished. The triumph over wickedness was realized not by an act of judgment but through the suffering of the Lion of the tribe of Judah, through the Lamb who was slain. What do believers do as they live in Babylon, as they live in a world in which the governments of the world are like ravenous beasts tearing apart the church? John tells us that we are to stay close to Christ, that we must not compromise with evil, that we must endure to the end, and that we must look to the final reward. The book of Revelation is not a prophecy chart about the future but a call to be a disciple of Jesus. John tells us to be faithful and fruitful, and we should not give in to despair, for in the end, all will be well.

Before we dive into the theology of Revelation, a brief word needs to be said about the historical context of Revelation and about the kind of literature we find in the book. When we read an ancient book (and modern books too!), it helps to know the circumstances that accompanied the book's writing so that we can place it in its historical context. In the same way, we are also assisted when we grasp the genre of a writing. Is Revelation narrative, poetry, an epistle, or something else? If we read a poem or proverb as if it is an epistle, we are bound to misinterpret it. We need to set the scene, then, before we consider the message of the book, and the theology will then be explained in the subsequent chapters.

Historical Setting

When we read the book of Revelation, we are struck by the vagueness of its historical setting. Despite the various claims of scholars, nothing in the book itself indisputably points to life under a particular emperor, whether we think of Nero (r. AD 54–68), Domitian (r. AD 81–96), Trajan (r. AD 98–117), or some other emperor. Such a state of affairs suggests that we should not rigidly tie our interpretation of the letter to any particular period or to the actions of a specific emperor. Obviously, the book was written at a particular time and addressed to churches in Asia Minor, but we lack definitive evidence for positing a specific date. I am not rejecting the attempt to posit a particular date. I will argue, in fact, for a late date shortly and will happily appeal to such to confirm interpretations offered here and there. The point being made is that no interpretation should be accepted that *demands* a particular date— an important hermeneutical conclusion that we can draw from the imprecision of the historical situation. Any interpretation that *requires* a particular historical setting imposes constraints in reading the book that can't be verified. In other words, we must avoid the rabbit hole of binding our view of Revelation to a particular historical reconstruction.

Still, if any date is chosen, it most likely falls in the reign of Domitian (AD 81–96). Irenaeus wrote about this matter late in the second century:

We therefore will not take the risk of making any positive statement concerning the name of Antichrist. For if it had been necessary for his name to have been announced clearly, at the present time, it would have been spoken by him who also saw the Revelation; for it was not even seen a long time ago, but almost in our own generation toward the end of the reign of Domitian.[3]

Irenaeus's meaning is contested, and his words don't indubitably point to the time of Domitian, but the most natural reading suggests

---

3   Cited in Eusebius, *Ecclesiastical History*, trans. Kirsopp Lake, LCL 153, 265 (Cambridge, MA: Harvard University Press, 1992–1994), 5.8.6; see also 3.18.3.

that John penned Revelation while Domitian was the emperor.[4] The subject of the verb "was seen" if the book is claimed to be written before AD 70 could be "him" (i.e., John). If that is the case, Irenaeus does not specify when Revelation was written but records when John himself was last seen. Such a reading is possible, but seeing John as the subject of the verb is quite awkward, and the syntax reads more naturally if the subject is the revelation that John saw on Patmos. The English translation cited here supports this reading by supplying the subject "it." The earliest external evidence, then, supports a date during Domitian's reign.

The remaining evidence we have from early tradition seems to support a later date, although in some instances the tradition itself lacks clarity. Clement of Alexandria (ca. AD 155–215) remarks that John returned from the isle of Patmos "after the tyrant was dead."[5] The tyrant could possibly be Nero, and thus it is possible that Clement supports an early date. But since the remainder of the tradition points us in another direction, it seems probable that the tyrant Clement had in mind was Domitian. In support of such a conclusion, Eusebius identifies the emperor as Domitian,[6] concurring with the most natural reading of Irenaeus. Victorinus also traces the book to the reign of Domitian:

> When John saw this revelation, he was on the island of Patmos, having been condemned to the mines by Caesar Domitian. There, it seems, John wrote Revelation, and when he had already become aged, he thought that he would be received into bliss after his suffering. However, when Domitian was killed, all of his decrees were made null and void. John was, therefore, released from the mines,

---

4   G. K. Beale, *The Book of Revelation: A Commentary on the Greek Text*, NIGTC (Grand Rapids, MI: Eerdmans, 1999), 19–20. Against Kenneth L. Gentry Jr., *Before Jerusalem Fell: Dating the Book of Revelation*, rev. ed. (Powder Springs, GA: American Vision, 1998).

5   Clement of Alexandria, *The Rich Man's Salvation*, 42, in *The Exhortation to the Greeks; The Rich Man's Salvation; and To the Newly Baptized*, trans. G. W. Butterworth, LCL 92 (Cambridge, MA: Harvard University Press, 1919).

6   Eusebius, *Ecclesiastical History*, 3.23.1.

and afterward he disseminated the revelation that he had received from the Lord.[7]

Jerome (AD 340–420) advocates the same background: "In the fourteenth year then after Nero Domitian having raised a second persecution he was banished to the island of Patmos, and wrote the Apocalypse."[8] The tradition, as far as we can tell, was unanimous in positing a late date for Revelation. It is possible, of course, that Irenaeus was mistaken and that subsequent sources relied on Irenaeus and did not have firsthand knowledge about when Revelation was written.[9] After all, the early writers in history are not entirely reliable and are clearly guilty of mistakes in some instances. We face again the problem that we can't specify a particular date for the writing of Revelation. If the tradition is mistaken, it is probably safe to say that Revelation was written somewhere in the period between AD 60 and 100. I incline, however, to the judgment that Irenaeus is correct on the dating of the book. After all, Irenaeus knew Polycarp, and Polycarp knew John, and thus the tradition has a clear line of succession. Still, we have to admit that certainty eludes us. To sum up, the internal evidence doesn't clearly point to a specific date, and the external evidence, if we assume it is reliable, points to a date when Domitian was the emperor.

Genre

Scholars have often discussed the genre of Revelation, with the apocalyptic genre taking pride of place. At the same time, they have also noted the seven letters in chapters 2–3 and the prophetic character

---

7   Victorinus of Petovium, *Commentary on the Apocalypse*, 10.3, in *Latin Commentaries on Revelation*, ed. and trans. William C. Weinrich, ACT (Downers Grove, IL: IVP Academic, 2011), 13–14.

8   Jerome, *Lives of Illustrious Men*, 9, in *Nicene and Post-Nicene Fathers of the Christian Church*, 2nd ser., ed. Philip Schaff and Henry Wace (Grand Rapids, MI: Eerdmans, 1969), 3:364.

9   Cf. Craig R. Koester, *Revelation: A New Translation with Introduction and Commentary*, AB 38A (New Haven, CT: Yale University Press, 2014), 66–67.

of the book. Revelation, in other words, contains a mixture of genres: epistolary, prophetic, and apocalyptic. Bauckham rightly says,

> Revelation is a literary work composed with astonishing care and skill. We should certainly not doubt that John had remarkable visionary experiences, but he has transmuted them through what must have been a lengthy process of reflection and writing into a thoroughly literary creation which is designed not to reproduce the experience so much as to communicate the meaning of the revelation that had been given to him.[10]

The epistolary character of the book indicates that John addresses the situation and circumstances of his readers, and thus the message of the book must be tied to the historical location of the seven churches. Since we have letters, seven of them, we are reminded that the book wasn't written as a general tract about the end of history but was intended for the churches in Asia Minor in the first century. The epistolary genre in the book reminds us that we should not indulge in what I call "newspaper eschatology" in reading the book. The book was written to readers who occupied a particular social location, and presumably they understood, at least mainly, what was written to them. The hermeneutical significance of this fact is massively important, for it eliminates the popular conception that modern readers interpret Revelation better than the original readers. Those who propose such readings practice newspaper eschatology and read the book in terms of current events. Actually, all who pay attention to such things realize that such a hermeneutical approach is arbitrary since the interpretations change as events transpire. The interpretation of the book, even if one adopted the approach of interpreting Revelation in accord with current events, is scarcely clear since the interpretation of Revelation shifts over time. It is wiser hermeneutically to locate the book in its

---

10   Richard Bauckham, *The Theology of the Book of Revelation*, New Testament Theology (Cambridge: Cambridge University Press, 1993), 3–4.

historical context and to interpret it in light of the situation and the world in which the first readers lived.

At the same time, the reference to seven churches also carries symbolic significance, which suggests that the book was written for all the churches as well.[11] In that sense, the message of the book applies to all churches throughout history. Still, as readers, we rightly focus on the historical situation in which the book was written to decipher the meaning, while also recognizing that the book has a wider significance for the church of Jesus Christ throughout the ages.

At the outset of the book, we are told that Revelation is a "prophecy" (Rev. 1:3). The book concludes with a flurry of references to prophecy (22:7, 10, 18, 19; cf. 22:6, 9). Thus, the claim that the book is a prophecy clusters at the beginning and the end of Revelation, and such an inclusio signals to the readers that the prophetic character of the book is key in understanding the Apocalypse. As a prophecy, the book should be read aloud and heard by the churches when gathered (1:3). The oral recitation of Revelation is a constitutive element of the church's worship, indicating that the words of the prophecy were considered authoritative. Indeed, John emphasizes in the strongest possible terms the divine authority of what he wrote, saying that those who add to what is disclosed will suffer the plagues threatened in the book and that those who subtract from the revelation will not partake of the tree of life and will be excluded from the holy city (22:18–19). John here echoes Moses when he impresses on his hearers that they must not add to or subtract from the commands given from Mount Sinai (Deut. 4:2), and the echo indicates that John believed his words were as authoritative as the words of Torah.

The content of the prophecy is discerned by reading the entire book, but John tells us that as a prophecy the book "discloses what must soon take place" (Rev. 22:6, my trans.). And at both the beginning and the end of the book, John declares one of the key elements of his prophecy: "The time is near" (1:3; 22:10), a theme that must be considered

11 So Bauckham, *Theology of Revelation*, 16.

in due course. Since we have a divine disclosure of what must occur soon, what is prophesied must be not sealed up but announced to the churches (22:10). The prophecy, however, isn't written merely to convey information; the purpose is ethical formation and transformation, since genuine hearing leads to obedience, to keeping the words of the prophecy (1:3; 22:7). The prophetic vision has a pragmatic purpose that is intended to shape the thinking and to transform the behavior of the readers. We could say in general terms that Revelation has a wisdom purpose, and by wisdom I mean that it is intended to shape the character of the readers.[12]

Nowhere does John say that he is writing a book in the apocalyptic genre, though the first word of the book is *apokalypsis* (Gk. "revelation"), which is probably intended to tell us something about the nature of the book. In any case, there is virtually universal agreement about the apocalyptic character of Revelation. Adela Yarbro Collins has consulted and included the work of John Collins, David Hellholm, and David Aune in proposing the following definition:

> *Apocalypse* is a genre of revelatory literature with a narrative framework, in which a revelation is mediated by an otherworldly being to a human recipient, disclosing a transcendent reality which is both temporal, insofar as it envisages eschatological salvation, and spatial, insofar as it involves another supernatural world. Apocalypse was intended to interpret present earthly circumstances in light of the supernatural world and of the future, and to influence both the understanding and the behavior of the audience by means of divine authority.[13]

---

12   Supporting such a general conception of wisdom is Jeffrey de Waal Dryden, *A Hermeneutic of Wisdom: Recovering the Formative Agency of Scripture* (Grand Rapids, MI: Baker Academic, 2018).

13   Adela Yarbro Collins, "Introduction," *Semeia* 36 (1986): 7. See the earlier definition proposed by John J. Collins, "Introduction: Towards the Morphology of a Genre," *Semeia* 14 (1979): 9. Apocalypse, he says, is "revelatory literature with a narrative framework, in which a revelation is mediated by an otherworldly being to a human recipient, disclosing a transcendental reality which is both temporal, insofar as it envisages eschatological salvation, and spatial, insofar as it involves another supernatural world."

Certain characteristics are typical in apocalypses, but the pragmatic, practical element should be especially stressed here.[14] David Aune describes the apocalyptic worldview to be "centered on the expectation of God's imminent intervention into human history in a decisive manner to save his people and punish their enemies by destroying the existing fallen cosmic order and by restoring or recreating the cosmos to its original pristine perfection."[15] Bauckham remarks that Revelation differs from other apocalypses in that the amount of visual imagery exceeds what we see in other apocalypses, and we don't have the longer conversations between the mediator of revelation and the one who receives it, which is quite common in other apocalypses.[16] As readers, we might wish for such conversations, for they would presumably solve some of the interpretive puzzles that bedevil us.

We should note, by the way, that apocalyptic isn't restricted to the book of Revelation. We see apocalyptic sections in parts of Isaiah, Ezekiel, and Zechariah in the Old Testament. John is also informed by Jesus's eschatological discourse in Matthew 24–25 (cf. Mark 13; Luke 21) as well. We also have apocalyptic writings in Second Temple Jewish literature (e.g., 1 Enoch, 4 Ezra, 2 Baruch), and so readers of Revelation would, assuming they were familiar with some of these other writings, not find Revelation to be completely foreign or a radically new way of writing.

The book contains a revelation communicated in a narrative that rehearses the Lord's triumph over the forces of evil, as we are informed

---

14 Christopher Rowland says about apocalyptic, "We ought not to think of apocalyptic as being primarily a matter of either a particular literary type or distinctive subject-matter, though common literary elements and ideas may be ascertained. Rather, the common factor is the belief that God's will can be discerned by means of a mode of revelation which unfolds directly the hidden things of God. To speak of apocalyptic, therefore, is to concentrate on the theme of the direct communication of the heavenly mysteries in all their diversity." *The Open Heaven: A Study of Apocalyptic in Judaism and Early Christianity* (New York: Crossroad, 1982), 14.

15 David E. Aune, "Apocalypticism," in *Dictionary of Paul and His Letters*, ed. Gerald F. Hawthorne, Ralph P. Martin, and Daniel G. Reid (Downers Grove, IL: InterVarsity Press, 1993), 25.

16 Bauckham, *Theology of Revelation*, 9–10.

about the end of history and the coming new heavens and new earth. To use Yarbro Collins's terms, an "otherworldly being"—that is, an angel—communicated the revelation to a "human recipient," namely, John. We have a transcendent reality, a heavenly perspective of what is taking place on earth, and yet the story is also linear in that it forecasts the final outcome of events taking place on earth. John clearly interprets in his visions the events occurring on earth, informing us about evil and good from a heavenly perspective so that believers will refuse to join forces with evil and will persevere in faith and hope until the end. Brian Tabb says that apocalypses have two purposes: (1) "to encourage and comfort believers" in their suffering and (2) to "challenge believers to adopt a new perspective on reality" in light of the end.[17] I would add that in Revelation the readers are exhorted to remain faithful to God and Christ, to endure until the final day by not capitulating to the pressures imposed on them from the world.

Apocalyptic typically has certain characteristics, and a helpful resource in this regard is Leon Morris's book *Apocalyptic*.[18] The list below captures some of the characteristics:

historical dualism
visions
pseudonymity (Revelation excepted)
symbolism
numerology
angelology
demonology
predicted woes

If we consider how the book of Revelation relates to this list, we see that it fits quite nicely. We don't have ontological dualism, in which God and Satan are equally powerful, but we do have historical dualism, in which

17 Brian J. Tabb, *All Things New: Revelation as Canonical Capstone*, NSBT 48 (Downers Grove, IL: IVP Academic, 2019), 5.
18 Leon Morris, *Apocalyptic*, 2nd ed. (Grand Rapids, MI: Eerdmans, 1972).

there is a cosmic conflict between God and Satan. We also recognize that much of the book stems from visions John received, which are then communicated to his readers. Many apocalypses, such as 1 Enoch or 4 Ezra, are obviously pseudonymous, but Revelation stands out as an exception, as virtually all scholars agree, in identifying John as the author. Scholars aren't agreed about the identity of John, but they do agree that the book stands out as an exception to other apocalypses in not being pseudonymous.

The symbolism of Revelation is indisputable, and we don't have to weary ourselves with listing all the examples. Vern Poythress says that in interpreting Revelation, we need to take into account four levels: (1) the *linguistic level*, which consists of the words John wrote; (2) the *visionary level*, which includes the visions John received, whether of beasts, dragons, lambs, or other elements; (3) the *referential level*, where the historical referent of the vision is unpacked so that the first beast may refer to Rome or the Lamb to Christ; and (4) the *symbolical level*, where the meaning of the referent is conveyed.[19] For our purposes we can collapse the categories into two: the visions recorded and the referent/meaning of the visions. For example, John sees Jesus as the Son of Man with a two-edged sword in his mouth (Rev. 1:16), and the sword stands for the power and efficacy of his word. Similarly, the enemies of the people of God are not literally beasts (Rev. 13); rather, the reference to beasts represents the devastation and tyranny imposed by Rome and the imperial priesthood. Again, Satan is no literal dragon with seven heads and ten horns (12:3), but mythological language about dragons communicates that the devil is terrifyingly powerful. Along the same lines, there are "seven spirits of God" (3:1), a phrase that almost certainly refers to the Holy Spirit, the number seven symbolizing the perfection and fullness of the Spirit (1:4). So too the 144,000 from the tribes of Israel figuratively describes the people of God since we have 12 x 12 x 1,000. The wall of the coming

---

19   Vern S. Poythress, "Genre and Hermeneutics in Revelation 20:1–6," *JETS* 36, no. 1 (1993): 41–54.

Jerusalem is 144 cubits, which is again 12 x 12, symbolizing the safety
and security of the people of God (21:17). So too the city being 12,000
stadia is obviously figurative since the city is larger than the entire
country of Israel (21:16).

Angels also play a prominent role in Revelation. We have already
seen that an angel conveyed God's message to John (1:1; 22:8, 9). At
the same time, the devil and demons often crop up in the book as
well. Finally, predicted woes are found in the seal (6:1–17; 8:1–5),
trumpet (8:6–9:21; 11:15–19), and bowl judgments (16:1–21). And
the judgments that will be unleashed on the earth aren't restricted to
these passages.

Since Revelation is identified as a prophecy but is also apocalyptic,
George Ladd rightly suggested some time ago that we don't need to
decide between prophetic and apocalyptic, though the focus in his article was not on the book of Revelation.[20] We have a mixture of genres
in Revelation; the book is epistolary, prophetic, and apocalyptic. But
here I will make a comment about the apocalyptic character of the
book. Why did John use this genre? It has often been pointed out that
apocalyptic appeals to the imagination with its symbolic pictures and
lurid images. The arresting images and depictions capture the minds
and hearts of readers, as they confront the world with new lenses. John
introduces the readers to a new dimension, a dimension of reality that
is inaccessible to those in the space-time universe. We could say that
Revelation is John's apocalyptic metanarrative in which he declares
to the addressees what is truly happening in heaven and on earth. As
Bauckham says, John "expand[s] his readers' world, both spatially (into
heaven) and temporally (into the eschatological future), or, to put it
another way, to open their world to divine transcendence."[21]

Said differently, John is revealing the true nature of things. To the
human eye, Rome with its empire is a superpower, and John doesn't
dispute the harsh reality of life on earth, but he also reveals the over-

20 George Eldon Ladd, "Why Not Prophetic-Apocalyptic?," *JBL* 76, no. 3 (1957): 192–200;
see also Beale, *Revelation*, 37–43; Bauckham, *Theology of Revelation*, 5–6.
21 Bauckham, *Theology of Revelation*, 7.

arching reality. We aren't confined to what is empirically obvious about Rome and its rule over the world. John unveils a divine perspective, and thus he tells us that the empire is from God's vantage point a ravaging and idolatrous animal and that its power comes from Satan (Rev. 13:1–18). So too the city of Rome is rich, dazzling, and exciting, but when we see reality from the standpoint of heaven, when we see the apocalyptic reality, it is evident that Rome is actually a whore and that all who get in bed with her are destined for judgment. The apocalyptic genre, then, opens readers up to the true reality of what is going on, to a heavenly and transcendent perspective.

Conclusion

I have suggested that Revelation is written near the end of the first century when Domitian was in power, and the churches in Asia Minor were facing persecution from the Roman Empire and the society in which they lived. The book is a combination of genres so that it has epistolary features but is also prophetic-apocalyptic. The apocalyptic genre is especially important in interpreting the book because we must see the symbolism informing the work. Otherwise, we are apt to misread what the author teaches us. The apocalyptic nature of the book teaches us that what is happening in history is awesomely important, that a cosmic conflict between God and Satan is underway. Believers must side with God and refrain from throwing in their lot with evil, for a reward that exceeds their wildest dreams awaits those who are faithful.

1

The Deafness of Those Living on Earth

IN THIS CHAPTER WE CONSIDER those in Revelation who refuse to hear the truth, those who close their ears to the message about Jesus Christ. John tells us about the earth dwellers, the beast, the false prophet, and Babylon. Readers need to know the truth about what is happening in the world, which means that they need to be aware of what they are up against. The true nature of the opposition must be disclosed to them.

An apocalyptic revelation discloses the true state of affairs, giving us a window into the transcendent reality that is hidden from us. John received via an angel a vision of reality that represents God's perspective on life, and in that sense we have a metanarrative—a heavenly disclosure about life on earth. We see in the book a great battle, a cosmic conflict between heaven and earth, between God and Satan, between believers and the beast, between believers and earth dwellers, and between the bride of the Lamb and the whore of Babylon. Life on earth may look ordinary, but for those who have eyes to see, for those who *hear* the revelation communicated to John, they see and hear about truth from another dimension, which represents the truth about life, death, evil, and goodness. When John talks about hearing, he is not the first to do so. We see the same theme in the Gospels. As G. K. Beale says,

John's repeated use of the hearing formula is thus not novel but in line with the prior prophetic pattern. John's use of the phrase "the

one having ears, let him hear" is linked to Isaiah 6:9–10, as well as to
Ezekiel 3:27 (*cf.* Ezek. 12:2), and is a development of the Gospels' use
of the phrase (*e.g.* Matt. 13:9–17, 43), which itself builds on Isaiah
6:9–10. As also in the case of the Old Testament prophets and Jesus,
the expression about hearing indicates that parabolic communication
has the dual purpose of opening the eyes of the true remnant but
blinding counterfeit members of the covenant community.[1]

Earth Dwellers

John describes those who are aligned with the beast, those who oppose
believers, as "those who dwell on earth" (Rev. 3:10, Gk. *hoi katoikountes
epi tēs gēs*). The phrase is a technical term in Revelation for unbelievers,
and they are called earth dwellers because they hear and see the message
that comes from this world instead of hearing the message that comes
from above, the message that comes from heaven. Only those who are
earth dwellers will face the judgment that will engulf the entire world
according to Revelation 3:10. The promise of preservation for believers
doesn't mean that they will be absent from the earth when the great
trial arrives; it means that they won't face judgment, that they will be
spared from God's wrath, just as Israel was exempted from the plagues
that devastated Egypt. Earth dwellers think that they live an ordinary
life, buying and selling, marrying and burying. John declares, however,
that "with the wine of [the great prostitute's] sexual immorality the
dwellers on earth have become drunk" (17:2). The woman with whom
they have committed sexual immorality is Babylon, which stands for
the city of Rome and the city of man in general.[2] Sexual immorality
(Gk. *porneuō*) doesn't refer to sexual sin but stands for idolatry, for the
worship of other gods besides the Lord. Israel in the Old Testament was
to be committed to the Lord, as a bride is faithful to her husband. The
Old Testament prophets declaim against Israel, lamenting her harlotry

1   G. K. Beale, "Revelation (Book)," in *New Dictionary of Biblical Theology*, ed. T. Desmond
Alexander and Brian S. Rosner (Downers Grove, IL: InterVarsity Press, 2000), 361–62.
2   See Brian J. Tabb, *All Things New: Revelation as Canonical Capstone*, NSBT 48 (Downers
Grove, IL: IVP Academic, 2019), 164–58.

and whoredom. So too the fundamental problem with earth dwellers is false worship, the degodding of the one true God.

We see particularly in Revelation 13—the chapter about the two beasts—the true nature of the earth dwellers: "All who dwell on the earth will worship it [the beast], everyone whose name has not been written before the foundation of the world in the book of life of the Lamb who was slain" (13:8). The earth dwellers don't represent all people on the earth; otherwise, all people without exception would worship the beast, which would mean that there would be no believers whatsoever on earth. Earth dwellers are described as those whose names aren't in the book of life. By definition they are unbelievers. They have given their allegiance to the beast instead of to the Lamb (see 13:12, 14). They are people of the earth instead of being a heavenly people.

Still, it is not as if earth dwellers fully realize the import of their actions; they are *deceived* in offering their worship to the beast (13:14). John gives us an apocalyptic revelation for those who have ears to hear about the true nature of earth dwellers. Presumably those who lived in the Roman Empire in John's day and who didn't believe in the Christ didn't think they were allied with evil. They were just getting along in the world as it was. Many of them probably thought they were virtuous and on the side of what was true, right, and beautiful. John, however, gives a heavenly and transcendent view of their lives, shining a spotlight on the ultimate commitment in their lives. They are astonished and dazzled by the beast instead of by the true and living God (17:8).

Since earth dwellers have given their worship to the beast and to the harlot, they oppose the proclamation of the gospel (11:10). The declaration of salvation and judgment is repugnant to them. Thus they cast their lot with those who put believers to death (6:10; 11:10). Obviously, many unbelievers, probably most, had no role in the actual death of believers. John, however, provides us with a radical apocalyptic vision of reality. Just as we see in the Gospel of John, so too in Revelation there is no neutral space. One is either light or darkness, in truth or in error, from above or from below (John 3:19–20; 8:23–24), from heaven or from the earth. Since the earth dwellers have given their lives to the beast and to the harlot, they will face judgment (Rev. 8:13).

The Beast

The terrifying earthly opponent of believers is christened the beast. The beast isn't mentioned until Revelation 11:7, and there we are told that it hails from the abyss, which signals that the beast is associated with the underworld, with death and evil. Indeed, the verse goes on to say that the beast makes war on the saints and puts them to death. We receive a fuller introduction to the beast in Revelation 13, and it is clear that the beast is Satanically inspired (12:17). The beast is compared to a leopard, a bear, and a lion (13:2). We have an obvious allusion to Daniel 7, where in night visions Daniel sees beasts coming up from the sea: the first is like a lion, the second like a bear, the third like a leopard, and the fourth indescribably horrible (Dan. 7:1–7). The Danielic interpretation clarifies that the four beasts are four kings and four kingdoms (Dan. 7:17, 23), and there is no need here to identify the four kingdoms from Daniel specifically, although all agree that the first is Babylon.

John sees the beast arising from the sea, and the choice of the sea isn't accidental since the sea represents chaos and surging evil (Rev. 13:1). In fact, the sea and the abyss in some instances in the Old Testament may designate the same place (Gen. 1:2; 7:11; 8:2; Deut. 8:7; Job 28:14; 38:16; Pss. 33:7; 42:7; 77:17; 107:26; 135:6), and the beast is said to come from both. Since the beast is described as a lion, a bear, and a leopard, combining together in one animal the first three beasts in Daniel, we have good reasons to think that the beast in Revelation signifies the fulfillment of Daniel's fourth and indescribably terrible beast. And most commentators have agreed that the beast represents the Roman Empire.

What is the significance of John describing the Roman Empire as a beast, drawing on Daniel? We have in both Daniel and Revelation one of the characteristics of apocalyptic, in which true reality is exposed and unveiled. The empire, John tells us, is not humane or conducive to

THE DEAFNESS OF THOSE LIVING ON EARTH   35

human flourishing. Instead, it is like a ravenous and ferocious beast that mauls, kills, and destroys human beings. Rome was extremely proud of its rule and government, but to borrow the language from 1 John, the empire was an antichrist (1 John 2:18). Richard Bauckham rightly points out that Rome is criticized not only because of its murder of Christians but because it trampled on the human rights and dignity of human beings in general.[3] As he observes, Revelation 18:24 indicts Babylon for killing not only prophets and saints but also "all who have been slain on earth." Rome almost certainly conceived of itself as fostering human flourishing, but the truth, John tells us, is that Rome is not only anti-God but antihuman.

Even though Rome deprived people of their rights, liberties, and even their lives, people stood in awe of the empire because of its unrivaled power. We have often seen in history that people support those who have power, even if that power is wielded unrighteously. The temptation to adore and to worship the strong is almost irresistible, and Rome could claim that it was "on the right side of history." The power of Rome is evident in the wound that the beast suffered (13:3, 12), and yet the wound was healed, suggesting a parody of the resurrection. The beast's wound and recovery probably signify occasions when it appears as if the empire's rule and power will come to an end, and yet out of the ashes the empire rises again. Many scholars think that the wound refers to Nero's death and to the rumors circulating about Nero's return. In support of such an interpretation, it is common to understand the gematria, the number 666, as a reference to "Nero Caesar."[4] Still, the solution isn't obvious since one has to transliterate Nero's name from Greek into Hebrew to come up with 666, and one wonders if believers

---

3   Richard Bauckham, *The Theology of the Book of Revelation*, New Testament Theology (Cambridge: Cambridge University Press, 1993), 38–39. So also G. B. Caird, *A Commentary on the Revelation of St. John the Divine*, HNTC (New York: Harper & Row, 1966), 223; Craig R. Koester, *Revelation: A New Translation with Introduction and Commentary*, AB 38A (New Haven, CT: Yale University Press, 2014), 711.

4   See, e.g., Bauckham, *Theology of Revelation*, 37; Richard Bauckham, *The Climax of Prophecy: Studies on the Book of Revelation* (London: T&T Clark, 1993), 384–452; Koester, *Revelation*, 538–40, 597–99.

in Asia Minor would have detected such a recondite solution. Even if the referent is Nero, the point remains largely the same. The empire that seemed to be collapsing rises again.

The incredibly difficult words in Revelation 17 also support the notion that a godlike authority and power was attributed to Rome. We read that the beast "was, and is not, and is about to rise from the bottomless pit and go to destruction" (17:8). John goes on to say about kings, "Five . . . have fallen, one is, the other has not yet come, and when he does come he must remain only a little while. As for the beast that was and is not, it is an eighth but it belongs to the seven, and it goes to destruction" (17:10–11). On the one hand, John says the beast "is not" (17:8), but on the other hand, he says that one king "is" in 17:10. Trying to put together these two claims is one of the great puzzles in the book—perhaps one of the most difficult in the Scriptures. Interpreters have tried to work out what John is saying by producing a list of emperors that match the eight kings or alternatively by constructing a list of eight empires. Without going into details, it is scarcely clear that any list of emperors or empires really fits, and the solutions seem forced and artificial. Thus, it is better to read the text more generally and symbolically. Grant Osborne is correct in seeing a reference to emperors, but at the same time, he understands the number seven symbolically, where the number seven signifies that the "the world kingdoms are complete."[5] Craig Koester says that "seven is a round number representing the beast's power as a whole."[6] The text is obscure since there is a sense in which the empire exists and a sense in which it does not. Osborne thinks a new king will arise who is not from the seven but will function like the former emperors.[7] Koester says, "The tyranny that has reared its head in the past might not be widely visible at present, but it is not gone; the beast's character has not changed."[8] The seven kings "represent the completeness of the beast's

5   Grant R. Osborne, *Revelation*, BECNT (Grand Rapids, MI: Baker Academic, 2002), 620.
6   Koester, *Revelation*, 691.
7   Osborne, *Revelation*, 620.
8   Koester, *Revelation*, 692.

power, rather than a precise list of first century sovereigns."[9] However we parse out the details, the resurrection of the beast[10] or its coming[11] leads people to worship, for the beast, in the estimation of the people, is incomparable, just as God is incomparable, and thus they exclaim, "Who is like the beast, and who can fight against it?" (13:4). People put their trust in the beast and praise it as a divine figure. The beast casts a spell over people, deceiving them because it speaks with a godlike authority (13:15).

The beast is radically narcissistic and self-obsessed, boasting of its exploits and reviling the one true god (13:5; cf. Dan. 7:8, 11, 20). The totalitarian impulses of the beast translate into rage against the one and only true God and his people (Rev. 13:6). Like all megalomaniacs, it doesn't merely elicit worship but demands and enforces homage (13:12). Earth dwellers are deceived and grant obeisance to the beast (13:14), whereas political, economic, and bureaucratic pressure is put on believers to give adulation to the beast (13:16–17). When they refuse to capitulate, they face economic discrimination and are put to death (11:7). The beast claims greatness, but John has a piece of numerological apocalyptic wisdom to convey about the empire. The beast's number "is the number of a man, and his number is 666" (13:18). The meaning of this verse, of course, has been debated intensely throughout history, and it would be presumptuous to claim certainty about its interpretation. I am convinced by the reading that doesn't lock onto a particular individual. It is common, as was noted previously, to identify the number with Nero, but this requires constructing numerology from Hebrew, which seems too clever and obscure for most recipients of the letter. What John tells us is more significant and striking. The empire that claims to be divine is merely human; the number 666 falls short of the perfect number 777. In other words, the beast is human, not divine, and thus John tells us that all its pretensions to glory are laughable. The

9   Tabb, *All Things New*, 126.
10   So G. K. Beale, *The Book of Revelation: A Commentary on the Greek Text*, NIGTC (Grand Rapids, MI: Eerdmans, 1999), 875–76.
11   Bauckham, *Climax of Prophecy*, 407.

beast rules in totalitarian fashion, oppressing those who resist it. Pitirim
Sorokin (1889–1968), a Russian-American sociologist, describes well
the society that develops under totalitarian rule:

> Inalienable rights will be alienated; Declarations of Rights either abol-
> ished or used only as beautiful screens for an unadulterated coercion.
>   Governments will become more and more hoary, fraudulent, and
> tyrannical, giving bombs instead of bread; death instead of freedom;
> violence instead of law. . . .
>   Security of life and possessions will fade. With these, peace of
> mind and happiness. Suicide, mental disease, and crime will grow.[12]

John teaches that the rule of the beast continues to manifest itself in
human history. The beast that seemed to be dethroned marches on, and
people prostrate themselves before the one who seems all-powerful.

The Second Beast

The second beast is the sidekick of the first (Rev. 13:11–18), and since
it is also called a beast, it has the same destructive and ravaging character. We receive further illumination when the beast is described as
"the false prophet" (16:13; 19:20; 20:10). The second beast, then, has
a religious and prophetic dimension, showing that political power is
intertwined with religious devotion so that there is no separation of
church and state. The historical reference likely represents "the priesthood of the imperial cult."[13] The second beast parodies Christ since it
has two horns like a lamb (13:11). As the false prophet, the second beast

---

12 Pitirim Sorokin, *Social and Cultural Dynamics: A Study of Change in Major Systems of
    Art, Truth, Ethics, Law and Social Relationships* (1937; repr., Abingdon, UK: Taylor &
    Francis, 2017), chap. 40, Google Books.
13 S. R. F. Price, *Rituals and Power: The Roman Imperial Cult in Asia Minor* (Cambridge:
    Cambridge University Press, 1984), 197. Cf. Caird, *Revelation*, 17; Bauckham, *Theology of
    Revelation*, 38; Bauckham, *Climax of Prophecy*, 446; Robert H. Mounce, *The Book of Revela-
    tion*, NICNT (Grand Rapids, MI: Eerdmans, 1977), 259. Beale suggests the priesthood
    of the imperial cult or political authorities who enforced emperor worship. *Revelation*,
    717. Osborne doesn't limit the reference to the imperial cult. *Revelation*, 510.

"deceives" those who worship the beast and receive its image (19:20) by performing spectacular signs that dazzle observers (13:13–15; 19:20). We are reminded of Deuteronomy 13:1–3:

> If a prophet or a dreamer of dreams arises among you and gives you a sign or a wonder, and the sign or wonder that he tells you comes to pass, and if he says, "Let us go after other gods," which you have not known, "and let us serve them," you shall not listen to the words of that prophet or that dreamer of dreams. For the LORD your God is testing you, to know whether you love the LORD your God with all your heart and with all your soul.

We see again the role of apocalyptic revelation. The "evidence" seems to attest the validity of the message proclaimed by the false prophet, but evidence must always be interpreted within the matrix of divine revelation, particularly in light of the truth that one must worship only the one true God. We also noticed previously the totalitarian and coercive nature of the power exercised by the two beasts (Rev. 13:16–17). We do not find a "live and let live" world; instead, the second beast discriminates against those who don't prostrate themselves before the beast. Political tyranny, economic discrimination, and religious persecution mark the rule of the two beasts.

Babylon the Harlot

The jealous competitor of the bride of the Lamb is Babylon. Obviously, the moniker Babylon is symbolic, for virtually no commentator thinks that John refers to Babylon literally. The name stirs up the memory of Old Testament antecedents, among whom Babylon is the great enemy of the people of God. John tips the readers off regarding the identity of Babylon in informing us that the woman sits on "seven mountains" (Rev. 17:9), and "the woman you saw is the great city that has dominion over the kings of the earth" (17:18). Such information clarifies that the city is Rome, the capital city of the empire. As Osborne notes, the reference to Rome rules out a preterist view, at least a preterist view centered on Jerusalem, for the city is clearly not Jerusalem, and Rome wasn't destroyed until around four hundred years later.[14] The woman works hand in glove with the beast. Indeed, the beast supports and promotes her welfare in that she sits on the beast (17:3).

To the human eye, Rome was prosperous, rich, entrancing, exciting, and beautiful—"arrayed in purple and scarlet, and adorned with gold and jewels and pearls" (17:4)—a city pulsating with business and commerce, with entrepreneurs hawking their wares. Still, the city, like the beast, is a mystery (17:7), and John unveils for readers the true nature of the city. The city bustles with business and promises prosperity, but in reality the woman is a wicked prostitute (17:1, 4, 5, 15, 16; 19:2). Bauckham says about Babylon,

> At first glance, she might seem to be the goddess Roma, in all her glory, a stunning personification of the civilization of Rome, as she was worshiped in many a temple in the cities of Asia. But as John sees her, she is a Roman prostitute, a seductive whore and a scheming witch, and her wealth and splendor represent the profits of her disreputable trade.[15]

Babylon is the engine of economic oppression,[16] and both the kings of the earth and the earth dwellers have gotten into bed with her, engaging in sexual immorality (17:2; 18:3). We need to enter John's symbolic world to grasp what he is saying, for he enters the world of the Old Testament, where Israel's attachment to other gods is depicted as harlotry (cf. Jer. 3:1–3; Ezek. 16; 23; Hos. 2:5; 4:10–12, 18; 5:3–4; 6:10; 9:1).[17] Paul says that true worship consists of glorifying God and giving him thanks (Rom. 1:21). Babylon glorifies itself and lives for its own comfort (Rev. 18:7). Furthermore, she thinks she is unassailable in her

14 Osborne, *Revelation*, 628.
15 Bauckham, *Theology of Revelation*, 17–18.
16 See Mounce, *Revelation*, 251; Bauckham, *Theology of Revelation*, 35–36; Beale, *Revelation*, 684–85.
17 See Raymond C. Ortlund Jr., *God's Unfaithful Wife: A Biblical Theology of Spiritual Adultery*, NSBT 2 (Downers Grove, IL: InterVarsity Press, 2002).

rule, convinced that grief and sorrow will never be her portion since she is a queen (18:7). Doubtless, sexual sin is included in Babylon's sins, but the focus is on idolatry, the worship of other gods. Babylon is "the mother of prostitutes" (17:5), which probably means that other cities in the world imitate and follow the example of Babylon in their harlotry.

The woman Babylon may look stunning and beautiful, but she is actually demonic and unclean (18:2). The idolatry of Babylon is accompanied by—or perhaps better, expressed by—her material prosperity. Babylon was a shopper's paradise, where goods from the farthest reaches of the world were available (18:12–13, 16–17). The city was filled with astonishingly gifted musicians, skilled craftsmen of every trade, the best and tastiest food, and technological wizardry (18:22–23). But at the same time, its prosperity was gained unjustly, even enslaving other human beings to support her lavish lifestyle. Note how Revelation 18:13 concludes its list of Babylon's fine goods with slavery: ". . . cinnamon, spice, incense, myrrh, frankincense, wine, oil, fine flour, wheat, cattle and sheep, horses and chariots, and slaves, that is, *human souls*." Babylon's oppression doesn't end there but climaxes in the spilling of the blood of the saints (17:6; 18:24; 19:2). John describes the martyrdom of the saints in a dramatic way, depicting Babylon as a disgusting drunk who has imbibed the blood of the saints (17:6). We note again the apocalyptic perspective because in reality only some and not all believers were put to death in Rome. Still, John unveils the true nature of the city, its inner desires and motivations, which of course manifest themselves in actions. Thus, the harlot is pictured as dead drunk, holding a golden cup, the blood of the saints dripping down her lips.

The Dragon

Unsuspecting readers might be surprised to learn that the most common word for the devil in Revelation is the word "dragon," which occurs thirteen times, whereas the word "Satan" is found eight times, "devil" five times, and "serpent" four times. A dragon in the ancient world wasn't a creature who breathed fire and had wings and claws. The appellation "dragon" fits with the apocalyptic character of the book, for the enemy of the people of God is described in mythological terms as a monster who exercises a preternatural power over human beings. The symbol of the dragon or serpent was a common cultural convention. The Old Testament background includes references to Leviathan, Rahab, and Tannin (Job 3:8; 9:13; 26:12; 41:1; Isa. 27:1; 51:9; Pss. 74:14; 89:10; 104:26). John pulls back the curtain on reality and informs readers about a cosmic conflict, a heavenly war being waged on the saints from a source that isn't observable to human beings. The dragon takes center stage in Revelation 12–13, where the battle between the dragon and the people of God is featured.

The term "Satan," which means "adversary," designates Satan's influence on others. Twice, the Jews are identified as "a synagogue of Satan" (2:9; 3:9), which means that the Jewish synagogues in Smyrna and Philadelphia have turned against Christians, probably by reporting them to imperial authorities. In Martyrdom of Polycarp 12.1–13.2, which is dated sometime in the mid-second century, Jews reported Polycarp to Roman imperial authorities, saying that he was not willing to offer sacrifice or worship the emperor. Presumably the Jews wanted to distinguish themselves from Christians, arguing that the latter were not a legal sect, thereby exposing believers to discrimination, harassment, and persecution. Similarly, Pergamum is characterized as a place "where Satan's throne is," that is, "where Satan dwells" (Rev. 2:13). Most scholars agree that we have a reference here to the imperial cult, which demanded that Christians worship the emperor.[18] Those in Thyatira under "Jezebel's" influence (2:20) know "what some call the deep things of Satan" (2:24), which includes permission to engage in sexual sin and eat food sacrificed to idols (2:20). What is interesting is that references to Satan especially cluster in the letter to the churches and center on his attempt to subvert the faith of God's people either

---

18 Cf. Osborne, *Revelation*, 141; David E. Aune, *Revelation 1–5*, WBC 52A (Nashville: Thomas Nelson, 1997), 183–84. On emperor worship in Revelation, see Beale, *Revelation*, 5–12; Osborne, *Revelation*, 6–7. Koester thinks the reference is more general. *Revelation*, 286–87.

through persecution or by drawing believers into compromise. We also see two instances of the term "Satan" in chapter 20 (20:2, 7; cf. 12:9), where we are reminded that he is the adversary of the people of God.

The term "devil" is found five times (2:10; 12:9, 12; 20:2, 10), and again chapters 12 and 20 are the most prominent. The word "devil" means "slanderer," and that fits with the claim that he accuses the people of God (12:10). John, in fact, emphasizes his role in deceiving human beings about the truth (12:9; 20:10). The devil is also characterized as full of fury and irrational anger toward God and his people (12:12), and that fury manifests itself especially in persecution, though he uses human agents, such as Roman authorities, to work out his designs. The devil is identified as "the serpent" four times (12:9, 14, 15; 20:2). Again, chapter 12 is the most prominent. Twice he is called "that ancient serpent" (12:9; 20:2), which clearly alludes to Genesis 3, where the serpent tempts and deceives Eve so that she disobeys the Lord.

The dragon's seven heads and ten horns symbolize authority and strength (Rev. 12:3). The sweeping away of "a third of the stars of heaven" (12:4), if we pay attention to the Danielic background, refers to his persecution of believers, for in Daniel the stars that are cast and trampled on the ground by Antiochus IV Epiphanes aren't angels but the people of Israel (Dan. 8:10).[19] Thus the account in Revelation 12 does not refer to an original war in heaven in which angels joined the devil in rebelling against God.[20] Just as the dragon persecutes the saints, so too he attempted to slaughter the Son, who was appointed to rule the nations as Messiah and Lord (12:4–5). We will return later to his war with Michael in heaven, in which he is cast out of the heavenly realms (12:7–9).

Since the dragon has been cast out of heaven, he knows his time to wage war is abbreviated, and thus he pursues believers with insane fury (12:12–17). The people of God are portrayed as a woman fleeing to the wilderness for safety, while the serpent pursues and persecutes

---

19 So Beale, *Revelation*, 635–36. For doubts about this identification, see Koester, *Revelation*, 545–46.

20 Against Osborne, *Revelation*, 461.

the people of God, attempting to destroy them with a flood. The referent of the flood is difficult to determine. Perhaps it is false teaching,
or more likely it represents everything the dragon does to seduce the
church, including false teaching, persecution, and miracles.[21] In any
case, the dragon's design hasn't changed since the days of Adam and
Eve, as he attempts to sever human beings from God. Revelation 12
ends on an ominous note. The dragon stands on the sand, looking out
to the sea, which represents the forces of chaos and evil (12:18). Out
of the sea the dragon summons his henchmen, the two beasts who will
advance his agenda in the world. The dragon and the two beasts are an
unholy trinity, a parody of the true Trinity. The dragon "had given his
authority to the beast" (13:4) to advance his agenda, which centers on
the dragon's desire to be worshiped and adored (13:4).

Conclusion

Life on earth may look ordinary and even plebian, but John reminds
readers that there is a war on, a cosmic conflict, a great battle between
good and evil, between God and Satan. Behind the opposition that
comes from the two beasts, Babylon, and the earth dwellers is the
great dragon himself, the ancient serpent, the great adversary and
accuser and slanderer of God's people. Just as he tempted Eve, so too
he is attempting to intimidate and to terrify the saints so that they
depart from God. The Roman Empire, the Roman religion, and the
great city of Rome are not neutral entities. They have thrown in their
lot with the dragon. Thus, what is happening on earth is not trivial
or insignificant. Believers must hear the message so that they truly
grasp what is going on in the world and so that they persevere until
the end and refuse to compromise with Rome. Unbelievers who are
on earth, whom John calls the earth dwellers, are an earthly instead
of a heavenly people. John in apocalyptic colors draws the line for
his readers: one is either on the side of the earth dwellers, the beasts,
Babylon, and Satan, or else one belongs to God. There is no neutral

---

21   Cf. Osborne, *Revelation*, 483.

space; either one hears the message proclaimed by the Lord, or one is deaf to the things of God. John writes so that his readers will hear and see what is at stake, so that they will be wise instead of foolish, devoted to God instead of to the dragon.

The message for us today is that we should not put our trust in political power to bring in the kingdom. This doesn't mean, of course, that Christians should forsake the political sphere, for we are called on to engage the culture and to do good in every sphere. But Revelation warns us about utopian dreams of bringing in the kingdom through political dreams. Indeed, as believers, we must be alert since the rulers of this world incline toward totalitarianism. Government may gobble up human rights in the name of justice, and Christians may find themselves in the situation described by John, in which they face discrimination in employment, are persecuted, or are even put to death. Such economic and political discrimination opens up the temptation to compromise with the world, and John warns believers about this mortal danger, which we will consider in more detail in the next chapter. We must not shut our eyes to the true nature of the battle being waged, nor should we be deceived, as if any political program will instantiate the kingdom of God.

The Saints Hear and Heed

HOW ARE THE SAINTS TO RESPOND to the cosmic conflict, to the
battle in which they are engaged? John tells them at the outset that
they must hear and heed his message, they must listen and obey, they
must pay attention and persevere (Rev. 1:3; cf. 22:6–7). We are not
considering in this chapter *how* the saints become part of the people
of God, for that subject is reserved for chapter 4. Here we attend to
what the saints are called to do, to their responsibilities as believers.
The saints are called to hear and to heed both in the seven "blessed"
sayings and in the repeated calls to conquer and overcome. Those
who truly hear conquer; they do what Jesus summons them to do.
They hear the message and don't throw in their lot with Satan, the
two beasts, and Babylon. They are faithful and endure until the end.
They obey what has been proclaimed, what they have heard, and they
do good works, which is what it means to truly listen to the Son of
Man, to the words of the Holy Spirit.

The Seven "Blessed" Sayings

It is fitting to begin with the seven "blessed" statements in Revelation,
which are listed below, and all the blessings point to the eschatological
reward. I will look at the reward dimension of these statements later,
but here we consider the implicit exhortation for believers.

Blessed is the one who reads aloud the words of this prophecy, and blessed are those who hear, and who keep what is written in it, for the time is near. (1:3)

And I heard a voice from heaven saying, "Write this: *Blessed* are the dead who die in the Lord from now on." (14:13)

Behold, I am coming like a thief! *Blessed* is the one who stays awake, keeping his garments on, that he may not go about naked and be seen exposed! (16:15)

And the angel said to me, "Write this: *Blessed* are those who are invited to the marriage supper of the Lamb!" (19:9)

Blessed and holy is the one who shares in the first resurrection! Over such the second death has no power, but they will be priests of God and of Christ, and they will reign with him for a thousand years. (20:6)

And behold, I am coming soon. *Blessed* is the one who keeps the words of the prophecy of this book. (22:7)

Blessed are those who wash their robes, so that they may have the right to the tree of life and that they may enter the city by the gates. (22:14)

It is no accident that seven statements of blessedness punctuate the book of Revelation, given the importance of the number seven in the book. The seven "blessed" statements point to a full and complete blessing, to a joy that overflows and satisfies. The Greek word for "blessed," as many have noted, is difficult to translate. Certainly, the blessing comes from God, and yet the word doesn't focus on what God has granted to believers, though it is doubtless true that all good things come from him. The word for "blessed" (Gk. *makarios*) could be translated "happy," but the English word *happy* is tied to circumstances and feelings in a way that does not accord with the term used here. Others have suggested that the notion is best expressed in terms of human flourishing.[1] It describes a state of well-being that comes from God. I will use the terms *blessed, happy, flourishing*, and *well-being* in the discussion below to describe what it means to be blessed, with the understanding that no single English word captures the meaning of the word.

The first "blessed" statement surfaces in the third verse of the book: "Blessed is the one who reads aloud the words of this prophecy, and blessed are those who hear, and who keep what is written in it, for the time is near" (1:3). Happiness, flourishing, and well-being will be the portion of both the reader and the hearers of the prophecy contained in Revelation. Still, hearing the prophecy alone is insufficient, for true hearing, as we see in the Old Testament as well, must lead to *doing*, to *keeping* the words of the prophecy. The eschatological dimension of blessedness is suggested since John grounds such well-being in the nearness of the end, which suggests participation in the final reward.

The second "blessed" statement doesn't occur for many chapters. In the midst of a text that warns believers about the unending torment that will be the portion of those who side with the beast, John calls for perseverance (14:9–12). He follows up this charge with his second statement about human flourishing: "And I heard a voice from heaven saying, 'Write this: Blessed are the dead who die in the Lord from now on.' 'Blessed indeed,' says the Spirit, 'that they may rest from their labors, for their deeds follow them!'" (14:13). The assertion contradicts our intuitions and experience since dying hardly qualifies as human flourishing or as a state of well-being! Paul identifies death as the "last enemy" (1 Cor. 15:26). Still, the divine voice from heaven affirms the blessed state of those who die, and the truth of the statement is so important that it must be committed to writing. Indeed, we have a double authentication as the Spirit attests to the same truth. We are not left up in the air, then, about the blessedness of those who die. It is

---

1   See especially Jonathan T. Pennington's discussion of the term in *The Sermon on the Mount and Human Flourishing: A Theological Commentary* (Grand Rapids, MI: Baker Academic, 2017), 41–67.

imperative to see that such happiness belongs to those "who die in the Lord," to those who are believers, and, in light of the previous verses, to those who have persevered in their faith until the end. The Spirit also promises rest to those laboring, which implies that after death they will experience peace and rest; the days in which they labor, toil, and suffer will come to an end. We find a similar conception of rest in Hebrews, where the writer promises heavenly rest to those who persevere in the faith (Heb. 4:9–10). Finally, saying that "their works follow them" (Rev. 14:13) also points to an eschatological reward that is given according to the works they have done. The "blessed" statement, then, is radically eschatological, focusing on the rest, the joy, and the reward that will be given to those who resist a society and culture opposed to Jesus's lordship. The blessing belongs to those who have lived according to the way of Jesus.

The third "blessed" statement is found near the end of Revelation 16, where the bowl judgments are rehearsed. The bowl judgments, as I will suggest in due course, occur near the end of history, and in fact, the verse after the "blessed" saying refers to Armageddon (16:16), which is the last war in history. In the midst of the ferocious judgments recorded in chapter 16, we read, "Behold, I am coming like a thief! Blessed is the one who stays awake, keeping his garments on, that he may not go about naked and be seen exposed!" (16:15). The seriatim rehearsal of bowl judgments is interrupted, and a word from Jesus himself is directed to the readers, reminding them that he is coming again and that his coming will be as unexpected as the arrival of a thief (cf. 3:3). The notion that Jesus's return will be like a thief echoes the Synoptic tradition (Matt. 24:43–44; cf. 1 Thess. 5:2). So too does the admonition to be alert and awake (*grēgoreō*), ready for his return (Matt. 24:42–43; 25:13), and in Matthew such readiness manifests itself in living a morally virtuous life, in refusing to allow evil to dominate one's life. John follows in the same train here, for those who are vigilant keep their clothing on and do not "walk"—that is, live—in nakedness so that their shame should be exposed. In Revelation defiled garments signify sin (3:4) and white garments faithfulness and righteousness (3:5; cf. 6:11; 7:9, 13, 14; 22:14).

Those in Laodicea are exhorted to acquire "white garments" so that "the shame of [their] nakedness" will "not be seen" (3:18). Nakedness, then, is another way of describing evil and its shameful character. The eschatological dimension of blessedness shines forth again, for those who live in a virtuous way will experience shalom and happiness when Jesus returns. The "blessed" statement looks ahead to the future, to the new creation that is coming, and implicitly exhorts believers to persevere in the present and to resist the allurements of the whore.

The final four "blessed" statements are clustered in the last four chapters of Revelation, which fits with the eschatological urgency that is ratcheted up as the book comes to a close. The statement in 19:9 comes after the judgment of Babylon is described in some detail (17:1–19:5). The saints rejoice over the judgment of Babylon, and they are also filled with joy because the wedding of the Lamb is at hand and because the bride has prepared herself for the wedding (19:6–7). Immediately before the "blessed" statement, we find a verse that echoes what we saw in 16:15; the bride is prepared because of her clothing. She wears "fine linen," "bright and pure," and the linen represents "the righteous deeds of the saints" (19:8). The "blessed" statement follows, where the angel instructs John, "Write this: Blessed are those who are invited to the marriage supper of the Lamb," and then says to him, "These are the true words of God" (19:9). Those invited to the eschatological marriage feast are flourishing and happy. The "blessed" statement is again tied to eschatology, and the context reinforces the theme that those who are blessed live righteously. The Lamb's blood qualifies people for the marriage feast, but here John stresses that they are full of joy because of their godly lives. Interestingly, as in 14:13, he affirms the truth of these words, for since the future world is curtained off from the experience of human beings, it seems unreal and even illusory, and the word of God confronts readers with reality. The promise of blessing is not a pious cliché but discloses the future world for saints.

The next "blessed" statement is in the famous "millennial" text in Revelation 20: "Blessed and holy is the one who shares in the first resurrection! Over such the second death has no power, but they will be priests of God and of Christ, and they will reign with him for a thousand years" (20:6). Many elements of this text can't be explored here but will be picked up later in a discussion of the millennium. The eschatological character of the text is unmistakable. Whatever the first resurrection is (whether it is reigning with Christ in heaven, the new birth, or the physical resurrection), it represents the life of the age to come. And those who enjoy such life will never experience the second death, which represents final and eternal death, torment in the lake of fire (20:14). Those who participate in the first resurrection will flourish since they will reign with Christ for a thousand years, whether that reign is in heaven or on earth. If we look at 20:4, we see another connection that has been present in all the "blessed" statements. Those who experience the first resurrection and avoid the second death sacrificed their lives for Jesus's sake. They refused to compromise with the beast and worship its image. John encourages his readers to persevere, to risk death, since their future happiness is rooted in their present faithfulness.

The sixth "blessed" statement has similarities with the first (1:3): "And behold, I am coming soon. Blessed is the one who keeps the words of the prophecy of this book" (22:7). The eschatological character of the text is evident again: Jesus is coming soon, and happiness and flourishing belong to those who keep the words of the prophecy mediated by John. The readers are to lift their eyes to another dimension, to another time, to the new world that is coming. Such a perspective will motivate them to obedience, to loyalty, or, as 22:8–9 says, to proper worship. Even glorious angels must not be worshiped, but worship is reserved exclusively for God.

The final "blessed" statement is in 22:14: "Blessed are those who wash their robes, so that they may have the right to the tree of life and that they may enter the city by the gates." We hardly need to say that eschatology is central since the happy ones are those who have access to the tree of life and who may enter the heavenly city, the new Jerusalem. John immediately launches into the sins of those refused entrance to the city, and moral categories and idolatry dominate (22:15). All seven "blessed" statements are eschatological, drawing a connection between the final reward and the new life believers live—their worship of the one true God, their utter devotion to Jesus, their refusal to align themselves with the beast, and their pursuit of goodness. Everything in their world and in their society beckons them away from trust in Jesus; the contemporary culture and all those who live on earth are against them. John reminds them that they are actually the flourishing ones, the happy ones, the ones experiencing God's shalom. They need to hang on until the end and receive the reward that is sure to come.

Conquerors

We have seen that blessedness is promised to those who hear and keep the prophetic message. Those who truly hear also keep, and if one doesn't obey, then one hasn't genuinely heard the message. A complementary way of describing the life of those who will receive an end-time reward is that they are conquerors or overcomers. Here we investigate the conquering statements in Revelation and attend to the context in which these sayings occur to discern what believers are called on to do. In the messages to the seven churches, the call to conquer is closely associated with the call to "listen to what the Spirit says to the churches" and is addressed to "anyone who has ears to hear" (Rev. 2:7, 11, 17, 29; 3:6, 13, 22 CSB). In every instance, except one (2:29), the call to listen sits right next to the admonition to conquer. Joyful hearing means that believers listen to the words of the Spirit, to the urgent admonition to conquer and emerge victorious in the cosmic conflict they face. They must not stop up their ears and refuse to hear the words of the risen Christ, the words of the Holy Spirit. Again, a list of sayings is helpful before investigating their meaning:

> To the one who *conquers* I will grant to eat of the tree of life, which is in the paradise of God. (2:7)

> The one who *conquers* will not be hurt by the second death. (2:11)

To the one who *conquers*, I will give some of the hidden manna, and I will give him a white stone, with a new name written on the stone that no one knows except the one who receives it. (2:17)

The one who *conquers* and who keeps my works until the end, to him I will give authority over the nations, and he will rule them with a rod of iron, as when earthen pots are broken in pieces. (2:26–27)

The one who *conquers* will be clothed thus in white garments, and I will never blot his name out of the book of life. I will confess his name before my Father and before his angels. (3:5)

The one who *conquers*, I will make him a pillar in the temple of my God. Never shall he go out of it, and I will write on him the name of my God, and the name of the city of my God, the new Jerusalem, which comes down from my God out of heaven, and my own new name. (3:12)

The one who *conquers*, I will grant him to sit with me on my throne, as I also *conquered* and sat down with my Father on his throne. (3:21)

And they have *conquered* him by the blood of the Lamb and by the word of their testimony, for they loved not their lives even unto death. (12:11)

The one who *conquers* will have this heritage, and I will be his God, and he will be my son. (21:7)

The Ephesian church (Rev. 2:1–7) is complimented for its endurance, its orthodoxy, and its works. Still, the Ephesian believers have moved away from the love they showed at the beginning of their Christian experience (2:4). Probably John includes both love for God and love for fellow believers because it is quite clear in 1 John that the two are inseparable (1 John 3:23; 4:20–21).[2] Nor is the defect of love a minor weakness; the church has plummeted remarkably, and they must repent or the church will be removed altogether and cease to function as a true church (Rev. 2:5). The call to conquer (2:7), then, means that the church must return to its first love, to a fervor for and devotion to the Lord that has slipped away, to a patience, kindness, and forgiveness that is no longer the lifeblood of the community. One must conquer and overcome to partake of "the tree of life," which is "in the paradise of God." The "tree of life" clearly signifies eternal life and entrance into the heavenly city (see 22:2, 14, 19), reaching back to the tree in the garden of Eden (Gen. 2:8–9, 10, 15; 3:22–24; 4:16), which is another name for paradise. In other words, those who don't conquer, those who don't renew their love, will not enter paradise at all; only those who conquer will eat of the tree of life.

The admonition is similar in Revelation 2:11, where conquering for the church of Smyrna is required to escape "the second death." The second death is later described as "the lake of fire" (20:14; cf. 21:8), and thus the second death signifies eternal death, final judgment from which there is no recovery. Conquering for those in Smyrna means being "faithful unto death" (2:10), not compromising with imperial power to sustain their lives. Since those in Smyrna must be prepared to die, the testing for "ten days" (2:10) isn't a literal period, nor does it mean that persecution will not last long. Ten days is symbolic for limited suffering confined to life in this world. We ought not to read this to say that the period of suffering in this life will necessarily be short, as if Jesus were insinuating that they would suffer for a short time in this world and then the rest of their lives in this world would be pleasant. We see a parallel in 1 Peter that is also addressed to a suffering church. Peter twice says that suffering will be for "a little while" (1 Pet. 1:6; 5:10). But

---

2   Robert H. Mounce, *The Book of Revelation*, NICNT (Grand Rapids, MI: Eerdmans, 1977), 88; Grant R. Osborne, *Revelation*, BECNT (Grand Rapids, MI: Baker Academic, 2002), 115–16. Craig R. Koester says that lack of love for other believers is in view. *Revelation: A New Translation with Introduction and Commentary*, AB 38A (New Haven, CT: Yale University Press, 2014), 269.

this "little while" is in light of the new creation that is coming, and thus the short time refers to life on this earth, to the entire period between Jesus's resurrection and return. So too John says that suffering is for ten days because in light of the new creation that is coming, the suffering is brief. Thus, believers are called on to endure martyrdom for the sake of Jesus Christ in order to receive an eschatological reward.

Conquering is also required in the church at Pergamum (Rev. 2:12–17). The reference to Satan's throne in Pergamum (2:13) is almost certainly a reference to the imperial cult since the city dedicated a temple to the divine Augustus.[3] The call to sacrifice one's life, which was the challenge given to the church at Smyrna, had become a reality in the life of Antipas, who was martyred, perhaps because he refused to compromise by participating in the imperial cult.[4] The church is commended for holding on to the faith in such a perilous situation. On the other hand, some in the church were propagating and practicing the teaching of Balaam by engaging in sexual immorality and by eating food offered to idols (2:14). Most commentators think sexual immorality refers to idolatry here,[5] and we have already seen that idolatry is described as adultery or harlotry in Revelation, and perhaps sexual sin isn't excluded.[6] We see in Numbers 25:1–2 that Israel ate sacrifices

---

3   On the imperial cult, see Dominique Cuss, *Imperial Cult and Honorary Terms in the New Testament* (Fribourg, Switzerland: University Press, 1974). For its role in Asia Minor, see S. R. F. Price, *Rituals and Power: The Roman Imperial Cult in Asia Minor* (Cambridge: Cambridge University Press, 1984). In support of the cult playing a significant role in Revelation, see Allen Brent, *The Imperial Cult and the Development of Church Order: Concepts and Images of Authority in Paganism and Early Christianity before the Age of Cyprian*, VCSup (Leiden: Brill, 1999), 164–209.

4   G. B. Caird thinks mob violence may have led to his death. *A Commentary on the Revelation of St. John the Divine*, HNTC (New York: Harper & Row, 1966), 38. David E. Aune doubts a reference to emperor worship and doesn't see the imperial cult as playing a significant role in the book. *Revelation 1–5*, WBC 52A (Nashville: Thomas Nelson, 1997), 182–84. But see Osborne, *Revelation*, 141.

5   See, e.g., G. K. Beale, *The Book of Revelation: A Commentary on the Greek Text*, NIGTC (Grand Rapids, MI: Eerdmans, 1999), 250. Against G. R. Beasley-Murray, *The Book of Revelation*, rev. ed., NCB (Grand Rapids, MI: Eerdmans, 1978), 86–87.

6   Osborne, *Revelation*, 144–45. Koester thinks idolatry is most prominent. *Revelation*, 288–89.

offered to other gods and worshiped other gods, and such events were accompanied by blatant sexual sin (Num. 25:1–9); the same is probably true in Revelation.

Those who conquer will resist idolatry, or if they are compromising, they will repent and turn from such practices (Rev. 2:16). The "hidden manna" and "white stone" are two ways of describing the final reward (2:17), and it is difficult to track down the exact associations.[7] We see in 2 Baruch 29.8 a tradition that envisions "the treasury of manna" coming "from on high," and those who partake of it "have arrived at the consummation of time."[8] Perhaps it is connected as well with the hiding of the ark (which had manna in it), the ark being put into the new temple at the end of time (2 Macc. 2:4–7; 2 Bar. 6.7–9; 29.8; Sib. Or. 7.148–49). The manna, then, would be enjoyed at the end-time feast. White stones, signifying acquittal in court cases, were given to people who were honored.[9] So too the new name signals permission to enter the heavenly city. For instance, Zion will be "called by a new name" (Isa. 62:2) when the Lord vindicates her. We see once again that conquering isn't optional but necessary for obtaining eternal life.

Those who conquer in Thyatira (Rev. 2:18–29) are promised end-time rule with Jesus and will receive the morning star, a symbol that is difficult to identify (2:26–28). Perhaps what is intended is a reference to Venus as the first star in the sky, which signified sovereignty in Roman military circles.[10] Others think we have a reference to Numbers 24:17, where Balaam prophesies that a star will come from Jacob and rule.[11] Grant Osborne suggests that both notions are intended.[12] Believers will enjoy such rule if they persevere until the end (Rev. 2:25), even

---

7 See the clear survey in Osborne, *Revelation*, 147–49. Cf. Beale, *Revelation*, 252; Caird, *Revelation*, 42; Koester, *Revelation*, 289–90. On the background, see Aune, *Revelation 1–5*, 189–91. Osborne mistakenly sees a reference to the present as well. *Revelation*, 147–49.
8 All Apocrypha and Pseudepigrapha citations are from James H. Charlesworth, ed., *The Old Testament Pseudepigrapha*, 2 vols. (London: Darton, Longman & Todd, 1983–1985).
9 Koester, *Revelation*, 290.
10 Beasley-Murray, *Revelation*, 93–94.
11 Beale, *Revelation*, 268–69.
12 Osborne, *Revelation*, 168.

though the temptation to compromise is intense.[13] The church is also commended for its "love and faith and service and patient endurance" (2:19). Still, some are falling short in the same way as those in Pergamum since they have fallen under the influence of a false prophetess whom John symbolically identifies as Jezebel (2:20). They are eating food offered to idols and showing devotion to false gods. The prophetess Jezebel promoted the message that indulging in such activities is not wrong. The tolerance in the church demonstrates that the church has lost its moral compass. True love guards the supremacy of God in all things and doesn't countenance the violation of moral norms.

The church at Sardis (3:1–6) is full of self-esteem and self-congratulation, but actually, the church is "dead" (3:1). The church must wake up and shape up, or otherwise, Jesus will "come like a thief" (3:2–3). We have a probable allusion here to the history of the city because it was twice conquered by surprise attacks when opponents (Cyrus II in 547/546 BC and Antiochus III in 214 BC) scaled the supposedly unassailable walls and cliffs with their troops and took the city.[14] The specific failings of Sardis aren't recorded, but some lived in a way that was defiling (3:4). Those who conquer will wear "white robes," which symbolize the cleanness and righteousness of those who are godly (6:11; 7:9, 13–14). Those who conquer will never be blotted "out of the book of life" (3:5; cf. 13:8; 17:8; 20:12, 15; 21:27; cf. Phil. 4:3), which means that only those who conquer will enjoy eternal life. The same truth is communicated by Jesus when he says that those who overcome will be acknowledged by him before the Father and angels (Rev. 3:5). Similarly, Jesus claims in Matthew 10:33 that those who deny him before human beings will be denied by Jesus before the Father (cf. 2 Tim. 2:12). The life-and-death nature of what is at stake could hardly be conveyed in stronger terms.

The church in Philadelphia (Rev. 3:7–13) is commended for its works and perseverance and is instructed to stand fast and to hang on until

---

13 Cf. Koester, *Revelation*, 302.
14 Osborne, *Revelation*, 171–72.

the end. Those who persevere and conquer are promised that they will be pillars in God's temple and that the name of God and the name of the city of God, the new Jerusalem, will be inscribed on them (3:12). This language is obviously symbolic. We know from Revelation 21:22 that in the coming new Jerusalem, there will be no temple since the Lord and the Lamb are the temple. Saying believers are pillars in God's temple signifies that they belong to the people of God and that their place is secure. Both God's name and the name of Jesus are inscribed on believers, showing that they belong to the Lord and his Messiah and that they are safe in their care. Only those who persevere and those who conquer will belong to the heavenly city, the new Jerusalem, which is described in more detail in 21:1–22:5.

The church at Laodicea (3:14–22), like the church at Sardis, is deceived about its spiritual state. They think they are spiritually rich when they are actually spiritually impoverished (3:17). Things have become so bad that Jesus threatens to spew them out of his mouth (3:16); vomiting out of the mouth means that they will not belong to Jesus, that they will not receive any reward, that they will face the second death in the lake of fire. Thus they must listen to Jesus's advice, show renewed zeal, and turn from their wickedness (3:18–19). Jesus, so to speak, is knocking at the door, and they must open the door to him (3:20). In context, the invitation and call is not an evangelistic summons but a word for believers in Laodicea, calling them to repentance. Joyful hearing means responding to Jesus's urgent summons. If they are deaf, as the earth dwellers are, they will not conquer (3:21). If they don't conquer, they won't rule with Jesus or sit with him on his throne. Such rule with Jesus should not be construed as a reward above and beyond eternal life—a special extra for those who are particularly faithful. It is not as if they will lose out on a special reward but still end up enjoying eternal fellowship with Jesus. The reward described here, which is the message of the Spirit for all the churches, is for all believers, and thus the issue for those in Laodicea is whether they will eat with Jesus in the messianic banquet (Isa. 25:6; Luke 22:30; Rev. 19:9). If they don't overcome, if they don't repent, they will be separated from Jesus's presence forever.

The last two conquering texts are outside the seven letters to the churches. We see in 12:11 that the saints conquer through the Lamb's blood, and that theme will be discussed in due course. Here we want to notice that they conquered "by the word of their testimony" and because "they loved not their lives even unto death." We remember that John was confined to Patmos because of the "testimony of Jesus" (1:9), and martyrs were put to death for their testimony (6:11; cf. 20:4), which likely means that they faithfully confessed Jesus's lordship over their lives (cf. 12:17). Indeed, the willingness to sacrifice one's life matches what we already saw in the admonition to the church at Smyrna (2:10).

The last text stems from Revelation 21:7, where those conquering are promised that they will "have this heritage" and that they will belong to God as his sons. The inheritance refers to the blessings of the new heavens and new earth described in 21:1–5 and the water of life that will be given to the thirsty (21:6). Israel is God's son (Ex. 4:22; Isa. 43:6; Jer. 31:9; Hos. 1:10; 11:1), as is the Davidic king (2 Sam. 7:14). The blessing of sonship also belongs to believers in Jesus Christ (Rom. 8:14–15; 2 Cor. 6:18; Gal. 3:26; 4:26). Jesus is designated God's Son in Revelation 12:5 and the Son of God in 2:18. Once again, conquering and overcoming are required for an eschatological reward.

John impresses on his hearers the need to conquer. They must hear this message and not close their ears to the words of the risen Christ and the Holy Spirit. Too often, the pastoral impetus for the book of Revelation is neglected. John wrote the book for pragmatic reasons so that believers would continue to persevere in the faith and to obey when they endure suffering, when they are tempted to compromise, when they face the pressures of everyday life. The need to hear and to persevere continues in our day, especially when so many fall into easy believism and conceptions of grace claiming that obedience and perseverance are optional. Too often Christians tone down the gravity of the exhortations in Revelation and undermine the need for perseverance. The words in the seven letters represent the words of Jesus and the Holy Spirit, calling believers to overcome, to conquer, to endure, and to hold on to the faith until the end. We must not and cannot compromise by worshiping anyone or anything else, by capitulating to the norms of the society and culture in which we find ourselves.

Suffering and Perseverance

We see in a few other texts what it means for believers to hear and to heed. We must remember that John addresses churches facing suffering and persecution. We saw this clearly in the church at Smyrna and in Revelation 12:11, where believers are challenged to be faithful to death, to give their all, even their lives, for the Lord Jesus Christ. The words of Jesus ring out to them and to us: "Do not fear," even though the devil casts some into prison, where they will face death (2:10).

The times are perilous, as we see from the prayers of those "slain for the word of God and for the witness they had borne" (6:9). The persecution of the saints causes them to cry out, "How long?" (6:10). They are living in the midst of "the great tribulation" (7:14). What is meant by the great tribulation is a matter of considerable debate, but I suggest that this tribulation extends from the resurrection of the Christ until he comes again.[15] Similar controversy exists over the expressions "forty-two months," "1,260 days," and "a time, and times, and half a time" (11:2–3; 12:6, 14; 13:5). The background is found in Daniel, who refers to "a time, times, and half a time" (Dan. 7:25; 12:7), to "half of the week" (Dan. 9:27), and to "1,290 days" (Dan. 12:11). Some think that the designations in Revelation refer to a limited period before the end of history, others to a literal three-and-one-half-year period at the end of history. I suggest that it refers to the entire period of the church's existence between the resurrection and the return of Christ.[16] Why is this hermeneutically important? Revelation isn't describing the story of other believers in another time and place. The experience of believers throughout all history is recorded here, and thus believers

---

15 See Koester, *Revelation*, 421–22, 429.

16 See especially Beale, *Revelation*, 565–68. For further discussion, see David E. Aune, *Revelation 6–16*, WBC 52B (Nashville: Thomas Nelson, 1998), 609–10. John F. Walvoord sees it as a literal time period. *The Revelation of Jesus Christ: A Commentary* (Chicago: Moody Press, 1966), 178. Osborne thinks it is a short period near the end of history. *Revelation*, 414–15.

will face persecution and discrimination during this present age (Rev. 11:2). To put it another way, we along with all Christians throughout history are in the great tribulation.

The church is also described as "two witnesses" (11:3), which harks back to the Old Testament conception of two witnesses (Deut. 17:6; 19:15), and as the "two witnesses," the church proclaims the gospel to the world.[17] Many scholars understand the two witnesses to refer to two individuals, but Beale rightly gives reasons for thinking that the two witnesses refer corporately to the church.[18] First, the lampstands (Rev. 11:4) refer to churches (1:20), signifying that the church as it proclaims the gospel is the light of the world. Second, the beast persecutes the two witnesses (11:7), just as he does the church. Third, the entire world sees their death and resurrection (11:9–13), which fits with a reference to the worldwide church. Fourth, the 1,260 days accord with what is said about the suffering of the church in 11:2. Fifth, the role of the two witnesses harmonizes with what is said about the witness of the church elsewhere in Revelation (6:9; 12:11, 17; 19:10; 20:4).

The imperial authority, despising the church, persecutes it, makes war on believers, kills them, and conquers them (11:7; cf. 12:13). We find the same notion in 13:7, where the beast makes war on the saints and conquers them (cf. 12:17). The word "conquer" (Gk. *nikaō*) stands out since John often stresses, as we have seen, that saints must conquer to receive the final reward and to avoid the second death. But we are reminded here that words must be interpreted in context. John doesn't mean to say by the word "conquer" that the beast causes believers to apostatize. Conquering here has to do with persecution and putting believers to death, and we must avoid the mistake of concluding that the word "conquer" has the same meaning in every context. We could put it this way: the beast conquering the saints doesn't mean that the saints won't conquer and obtain eternal life.

---

17 See Eckhard J. Schnabel, "John and the Future of the Nations," *BBR* 12, no. 2 (2002): 247–48.

18 Beale, *Revelation*, 574–75; cf. Brian J. Tabb, *All Things New: Revelation as Canonical Capstone*, NSBT 48 (Downers Grove, IL: IVP Academic, 2019), 97–101.

The saints experience economic discrimination (13:17) since they don't consent to worship what the world worships. Rome, the Babylon of John's day, drinks the blood of the saints as it extends its material prosperity (17:6; 18:24; 19:2). John doesn't minimize the agony of suffering, reminding his readers "of those who had been beheaded for the testimony of Jesus and for the word of God, and those who had not worshiped the beast or its image and had not received its mark on their foreheads or their hands" (20:4). Bauckham rightly observes that all believers in Revelation are portrayed as martyrs, but we should not take this imagery literally as if all believers will be martyred; the point is that all must be prepared and ready to die for Christ.[19]

The call to perseverance, then, isn't an idle word but addresses a context in which believers are distressed and suffering. We understand the depth of John's words when he describes saints as "those who keep the commandments of God and hold to the testimony of Jesus" (12:17). John, in Revelation, emphasizes not faith but faithfulness. But if he is the same author as the Gospel of John, which I think he is, we recognize that believing in Jesus was fundamental to his theology. Still, such believing, which is implicit in Revelation, doesn't receive the same accent in the last book of the Bible. Here the focus is on what believing looks like in everyday life. John doesn't think believers are perfect, as our survey of the letters to the seven churches shows. Believers can stray in significant ways, but ultimately and finally, they must be characterized by obedience to God's commands and by perseverance. Perseverance should not be confused with perfection, but those who belong to God walk in the right direction. They give themselves to God and to Jesus Christ instead of throwing in their lot with the empire.

After relaying at the beginning of chapter 13 the rule and terrifying authority of the beast, where the emperor is portrayed as warring against and killing the saints, John pauses to admonish his readers.

---

19 Richard Bauckham, *The Theology of the Book of Revelation*, New Testament Theology (Cambridge: Cambridge University Press, 1993), 92–93.

He reminds them of the need to listen: "If anyone has an ear, let him hear" (13:9). They must pay heed to the apocalyptic revelation granted to them. The words that follow are somewhat startling:

> If anyone is to be taken captive,
>   to captivity he goes;
> if anyone is to be slain with the sword,
>   with a sword must he be slain. (13:10)

We have allusions here to Jeremiah 15:2 and 43:11, but the context in Revelation is dramatically different from Jeremiah because Jeremiah describes punishments for those in sin, while John refers to the suffering that believers must endure as they are faithful to Jesus.[20] John underscores that believers must be prepared for such suffering; they may be imprisoned or even put to death. John doesn't want them to be astonished or surprised at what lies before them. And thus, he closes the verse (Rev. 13:10) by saying, "Here is a call for the endurance and faith of the saints." Those who are forewarned are forearmed, prepared for the cosmic conflict, ready even to die for the sake of the Lord Jesus Christ.

Another motivation for perseverance emerges in 14:9–12. Here an angel threatens those who worship the beast and its image with the wrath of God, with eternal torment. We will return to this punishment in the next chapter, but what is interesting is that John turns and applies what he says to the saints: "Here is a call for the endurance of the saints, those who keep the commandments of God and their faith in Jesus" (14:12; cf. 22:11). We need to remember that these stern words about unending punishment are not sent to or read by unbelievers; John informs the saints about the destiny of idolaters. The eternal torment of unbelievers says something to believers if they have ears to hear. Contemplating the torment that never ends for idolaters motivates John's readers to endure and to persevere, for by holding fast and remaining faithful, believers will avoid the punishment to

---

20 Rightly, Osborne, *Revelation*, 505.

come.[21] Those who are invited to the marriage supper of the Lamb have lived righteous lives, testifying that they belong to God and that they have not thrown in their lot with the beast (19:8). They have faithfully testified to Jesus and have not worshiped the beast (20:4).

We see in the great white throne judgment that the book of life is opened and that all people are judged by their works (20:11–15).[22] One's name must be inscribed in the book of life to escape the lake of fire, and John doesn't emphasize here that it is those who have faith in Jesus who are in the book of life, though that is doubtless true. Here he focuses on the concrete evidence, the observable fruit that belongs to those in the book of life. The necessity of good works for final salvation is a regular theme in the New Testament (e.g., Matt. 7:13–29; Rom. 2:6–11; 1 Cor. 6:9–10; 2 Cor. 5:10; Gal. 5:21; cf. Ps. 62:12; Prov. 24:12), and thus it is surprising that some fail to see its importance and that some even claim that the necessity of good works is contrary to the gospel. Revelation 22:12 sums up this theme nicely when Jesus says, "Behold, I am coming soon, bringing my recompense with me, to repay each one for what he has done." Two texts show clearly that those who practice evil will be excluded from the heavenly city and the book of life. We find in 21:8 that "as for the cowardly, the faithless, the detestable, as for murderers, the sexually immoral, sorcerers, idolaters, and all liars, their portion will be in the lake that burns with fire and sulfur, which is the second death." A similar sentiment is expressed in 22:15: "Outside are the dogs and sorcerers and the sexually immoral and murderers and idolaters, and everyone who loves and practices falsehood." The two lists are quite similar, but there are some notable differences: the first begins with the "cowardly" and "faithless," which are not in the second list, while the second has the word "dogs," which is lacking in the first. Dogs signify those who are

---

21   Faith leads to faithfulness. Rightly, Osborne, *Revelation*, 541–42; cf. Aune, *Revelation 1–5*, 837–38. We don't have a reference to doctrinal content here—against Beale, *Revelation*, 766–67.

22   See Osborne, *Revelation*, 721–22; Beale, *Revelation*, 1032–33; Mounce, *Revelation*, 365–66; Koester, *Revelation*, 790–93.

unclean, whereas the saints are pure and wear white clothing (3:4, 5, 18; 6:11; 7:9, 13, 14; 19:8, 14).

Conclusion

As we will see, Revelation teaches that the basis of salvation is the redeeming work of Christ on the cross, but John also emphasizes the moral change, the commitment that marks out those who belong to God. He doesn't demand perfection, but there is a new direction, a new orientation, a remarkable change in those who belong to God. Those who are the Lord's will conquer and persevere in faith until the end. Their names are in the book of life because of their good works—not because their works are perfect, nor because they are the ultimate basis of their relation to God, but because their works testify that the God on the throne and the Lamb is their Lord. The saints are those who hear and heed, who listen and obey. They are the blessed ones; they are the ones who conquer; they are the ones who endure faithfully until the end and will receive a final reward.

3

The Declaration That God Rules on His Throne

THE WORLD LISTENS TO THE DRAGON, the two beasts, and Babylon, but it is deaf to the things of God—or better, it is deaf to God himself. John writes so that the readers hear the word of the Lord, so that they hear his voice. If they listen, they will understand in the midst of an evil world that God is sovereign, that he is holy, and that he judges the wicked and saves the righteous. I reserve salvation for a subsequent chapter and here focus on God's sovereignty, holiness, and judgment. We saw in the previous chapter that believers must conquer, persevere, and remain faithful, and they will do so only if they hear the truth about God. John reminds the churches that the Lord God is the sovereign one, ruling and reigning over all history; he has not lost control in the midst of the chaos. The one who rules is also perfectly good, infinitely holy and righteous, and full of beauty. As the sovereign Holy One, the Lord will judge evil, condemning forever those who have refused to listen to his voice. Actually, the Lord speaks to unbelievers in the judgments that precede the final judgments, but many of the wicked refuse to listen and will experience the final judgment to come.

God's Sovereignty

The book of Revelation reveals both who God is and what he does, and perhaps the best place to start is the throne-room vision in chapter 4, where God is worshiped as Creator of all. The open door in heaven signifies that John is receiving divine revelation (4:1; cf. Acts 10:11). John sees a throne in heaven, which signifies God's sovereign rule over all (Rev. 4:2). The word "throne" appears in the singular forty-one times in Revelation, and thirty-seven of these refer to the throne of God. Clusters of the word "throne" appear in particular sections of the book: fifteen times in chapters 4–5, seven times in chapter 7, and six times in chapters 20–22. On thirteen occasions the word "throne" occurs with a form of the term "seated" (4:2, 3, 9, 10; 5:1, 7, 13; 6:16; 7:10, 15; 19:4; 20:11; 21:5), signifying God's settled authority. In every instance, God's throne is in heaven, communicating the truth that God reigns over all, and thus the suffering faced by believers doesn't indicate that God has lost control over the universe. It appears to believers as if Satan and the beast rule over the world, but in actuality, God rules over all.

The Greek word *edothē* ("it was given") occurs twenty-one times in Revelation, and in every instance it refers to what God allows to take place on earth. Sometimes what is given by God represents his gracious will, such as the white robe granted to believers (6:11), the pure and clean clothing for the saints (19:8), or the judgment over the world granted to believers (20:4). In many instances, what is given refers to the judgments God inflicts on the world for the evil perpetrated (e.g., 6:4, 8; 7:2; 9:3, 5; 16:8). John is informed by the Old Testament here. As G. K. Beale says,

> Not only does Revelation see the divine throne as ultimately behind the trials of believers and woes of unbelievers, but the major Old Testament passages formative for the visions of the seals, trumpets and bowls, without exception, portray God as the ultimate cause of the ordeals (so Zech. 6:1–8; Ezek. 14:21; Lev. 26:18–28 and their use in [Rev.] 6:2–8).[1]

---

1   G. K. Beale, "Revelation (Book)," in *New Dictionary of Biblical Theology*, ed. T. Desmond Alexander and Brian S. Rosner (Downers Grove, IL: InterVarsity Press, 2000), 357.

Most surprising are the instances in which God grants permission for evil to be done. For instance, the Gentiles are allowed to trample the holy city, that is, persecute believers for forty-two months (11:2). God's role in the rule of the beast also stands out. The arrogant boasting of the beast and its rule for forty-two months are permitted by God himself (13:5). Astonishingly, God even allows the beast to make war with the saints to conquer them by putting them to death (13:7). Indeed, the beast's authority over the entire earth is granted by God himself (13:7).[2] In the same way, the second beast's ability to do signs is bestowed by God (13:14), and God permits the second beast to grant "breath to the image of the beast, so that the image of the beast can both speak and cause whoever will not worship the image of the beast to be killed" (13:15). The passive voice of the verb *edothē* ("it was given") removes God *directly* from the evil that is perpetrated in the world, and thus John does not conceive of God as directly willing evil. On the other hand, evil doesn't exist apart from the divine will, as if it has an independent existence. Evil exists within the circumference of God's sovereign will. John's presentation of the role of evil is deft and complex. The evil actions of the wicked are truly evil, representing the authentic choices and decisions of those who pursue wickedness. God is not directly responsible for the evil that occurs, but neither does evil take on an independent status, as if it is unleashed on the world in a way that mystifies and puzzles God, as if even God himself doesn't exercise control over wickedness. God is sovereign over evil, does not himself commit what is evil, and yet permits the evil that takes place.

We find confirmation of the authority Satan has over the world elsewhere in the New Testament. The devil promises Jesus all the kingdoms of the world if Jesus will bow down and worship him (Matt. 4:8–9). Three times the Gospel of John designates Satan as

---

2   See G. B. Caird, *A Commentary on the Revelation of St. John the Divine*, HNTC (New York: Harper & Row, 1966), 167; Robert H. Mounce, *The Book of Revelation*, NICNT (Grand Rapids, MI: Eerdmans, 1977), 254; G. K. Beale, *The Book of Revelation: A Commentary on the Greek Text*, NIGTC (Grand Rapids, MI: Eerdmans, 1999), 695; Grant R. Osborne, *Revelation*, BECNT (Grand Rapids, MI: Baker Academic, 2002), 499.

"the ruler of this world" (John 12:31; 14:30; 16:11), and in his first epistle, John says that "the whole world lies in the power of the evil one" (1 John 5:19). Paul calls Satan "the god of this world" (2 Cor. 4:4) and "the prince of the power of the air" (Eph. 2:2). Revelation clarifies that God, in accord with his own mysterious wisdom, has given this authority to the devil. Thus God, not the dragon, is ultimately sovereign. The devil's rule over the world is derivative, authority that God has granted him.

It is fascinating to see that "the dragon gave" (Gk. *edōken*)—active voice—"authority" to the beast (Rev. 13:2). God's granting of authority to the beast is invariably passive (Gk. *edothē*), and yet it is clear that God has ultimate sovereignty over Satan. The active verb with reference to the dragon indicates that Satan stands behind the evil that is done directly so that the devil is morally responsible for the evil inflicted. God, on the other hand, stands behind evil indirectly and is not morally responsible for evil, even though evil could not occur apart from his will. We could say that God wills evil for a good purpose ultimately, although there are dimensions to what John says that are mysterious, particularly since John does not offer an explanation for God's allowing such evil to occur. It is clear in the narrative that the murder of the saints by the beast is a horrendous evil of which God disapproves, and yet by permitting such to happen, he wills its existence. Still, there is comfort in knowing that the dragon and the two beasts are not running loose in a universe sundered from God's will. He rules and reigns over all.

God's sovereignty and independence are also communicated when he is described as "the one who is and who was and who is to come" (1:4, 8). We have a clear allusion here to Exodus 3:14, where God discloses to Moses his name: "I AM WHO I AM." Much debate has ensued over the meaning of the phrase, but it certainly indicates the Lord's sufficiency, independence, and sovereignty.[3] In Revelation the Lord

---

3   For a survey of interpretation, see Brevard S. Childs, *The Book of Exodus: A Critical, Theological Commentary*, OTL (Philadelphia: Westminster, 1974), 50, 60–64, 85–87.

reminds believers that even in the midst of their current circumstances, he is Almighty God. Furthermore, he has always reigned as the Creator and ruler of all history since he is the one "who was." There never was a time when he did not exercise his rule over the world. And the future is also in his hands; he is the one to come, the one who will bring history to its appointed consummation. Interestingly, the order changes in Revelation 4:8, where the Lord is said to be he "who was and is and is to come." Perhaps the past is placed first here to emphasize in a particular way the Lord's reign over all previous history, to remind readers that God has always been Lord and King. In 11:17, God is he "who is and who was," and a reference to his coming is omitted since these verses describe his coming (11:15–19), the consummation of all history.[4] There is no need to say that he is the coming one in a text that emphasizes the wrapping up of all history. We can say the same about 16:5, where we find again that God is the one "who is and who was." Once again, the text describes the days of the final judgment, the days when all history will be completed and brought to an end.

God's rule over history is also communicated in the declaration "I am the Alpha and the Omega" (1:8; 21:6). The occurrence of this saying in 21:6 unpacks what it means by adding that the Lord is "the beginning and the end." The comprehensiveness of the phrases demonstrates that the Lord also reigns over every moment, every circumstance between the beginning and the end. The one who began all things and who will consummate all things rules over all things that come to pass. Thus, we are not surprised to find in 1:8 that the Lord is identified as the "Almighty" (Gk. *pantakratōr*), a term that is used eight other times in the book (4:8; 11:17; 15:3; 16:7, 14; 19:6, 15; 21:22). God reigns as the all-powerful one, as the awesome Creator and Sustainer of the universe, as the one who is working out all things for his own good purposes. Similarly, in 15:3, the Lord is identified as "King of the nations." The one who is Almighty rules

---

4   Rightly, Caird, *Revelation*, 141; Richard Bauckham, *The Theology of the Book of Revelation*, New Testament Theology (Cambridge: Cambridge University Press, 1993), 29; Beale, *Revelation*, 61.

over all for his name's sake; he is the mighty King and ruler over all peoples everywhere.

Revelation reminds a suffering church that God is the King of the ages, the ruler over all, and thus evil can't and won't triumph. Some contemporary Christians de-emphasize God's sovereignty when the topic of suffering arises. They have the laudable motive of separating God from the evil that occurs in the world. John in Revelation, however, while not charging God with doing evil, ratchets up the role of God's sovereignty. John doesn't believe the saints will be comforted by teaching them that God stands by helplessly as they suffer. Instead, the Lord reigns and rules over all that takes place in the world, and thus no suffering that strikes believers can take place apart from the will of God. John doesn't attempt to resolve the problem of evil philosophically, although as we have seen, he uses the passive voice in denoting God's role in the evil that takes place, demonstrating that God should not be held directly accountable for the evil that occurs.[5]

Beautiful Holiness

If we return to the throne-room vision in Revelation 4, we see the Lord seated on his throne, and his "appearance" is like "jasper and carnelian" (4:3). John records, "Around the throne was a rainbow that had the appearance of an emerald" (4:3). The language is obviously highly symbolic, and readers are reminded of Ezekiel's vision of the Lord in Ezekiel 1:26–28:

> And above the expanse over their heads there was the likeness of a throne, in appearance like sapphire; and seated above the likeness of a throne was a likeness with a human appearance. And upward from what had the appearance of his waist I saw as it were gleaming metal, like the appearance of fire enclosed all around. And downward from what had the appearance of his waist I saw as it were the appearance

5   For a helpful philosophical treatment of the question, see Guillaume Bignon, *Excusing Sinners and Blaming God: A Calvinist Assessment of Determinism, Moral Responsibility, and Divine Involvement in Evil*, PTMS 230 (Eugene, OR: Pickwick, 2018).

of fire, and there was brightness around him. Like the appearance of the bow that is in the cloud on the day of rain, so was the appearance of the brightness all around.

Commentators have attempted to find a one-to-one correspondence between the descriptions in Revelation and the attributes of God. The danger in such an attempt is arbitrariness and lack of clear evidence for the specific identifications proposed. John probably didn't expect us to be so precise in untangling the portrait given, intending readers to be affected by the general impact of the vision. John, like Ezekiel, uses such imagery in the attempt to describe the indescribable so that his readers will be struck with the awesome beauty of the Lord. The stones and rainbow emblazon on the readers' hearts the splendor and loveliness of God himself.

To put it another way, John doesn't focus on describing God himself but gives an indirect vision of him. As Richard Bauckham says, "The unknowable transcendence of God is protected by focusing instead on the throne itself and what goes around it."[6] We also see in the vision that the Lord is attended by the twenty-four elders and four living beings, which we won't linger to describe here. A massive thunderstorm is raging in the throne room, signifying that entering the presence of God is terrifying (Rev. 4:5). Such a reading is confirmed by the Old Testament background, for when the Lord descended on Mount Sinai, "there were thunders and lightnings and a thick cloud on the mountain and a very loud trumpet blast, so that all the people in the camp trembled" (Ex. 19:16). The sea of glass probably alludes to the expanse separating the waters in Genesis 1:7, and we also have an allusion to Ezekiel 1:22: "Over the heads of the living creatures there was the likeness of an expanse, shining like awe-inspiring crystal, spread out above their heads." Grant Osborne rightly says that "the emphasis is on God's awesome vastness, his transcendence and his holiness that separate him from his creation."[7]

6 Bauckham, *Theology of Revelation*, 32.
7 Osborne, *Revelation*, 231. See also Craig R. Koester, *Revelation: A New Translation with Introduction and Commentary*, AB 38A (New Haven, CT: Yale University Press, 2014), 363.

It is fitting, then, that the four living beings constantly exclaim, "Holy, holy, holy, is the Lord God Almighty" (Rev. 4:8). We are drawn back, of course, to Isaiah 6:3, where the seraphim exclaim,

> Holy, holy, holy is the LORD of hosts;
> the whole earth is full of his glory!

God's holiness designates his distinctiveness, showing that he is separate from all creation, that he is not to be trifled with. Certainly, he is holy because he is the almighty one, the Creator of all, the ruler of all the earth. At the same time, the evocation of Isaiah 6 and the subsequent narrative in Revelation 5, where we find no one worthy to open the scroll, show that the Lord's holiness consists in his infinite and matchless moral purity. It is frightening to enter his presence because, as Hebrews says, "our God is a consuming fire" (Heb. 12:29).

Thus when we come to the conclusion of Revelation 4, the worship that the four living beings and the twenty-four elders give to God accords with God's greatness and incomparability (4:9–11). The elders fall before the God who sits on the throne and worship him. They acclaim him as worthy to receive all "glory and honor and power" (4:11). He is worshiped because he is the Creator and sovereign of the universe, because it is by his will that all things have come into being. He is worshiped as the incomparably great God.

Perhaps this is the place to note the songs of praise that punctate the book, such as the song in Revelation 5:13:

> To him who sits on the throne and to the Lamb
> be blessing and honor and glory and might forever and ever!

We find a similar song in 7:12: "Blessing and glory and wisdom and thanksgiving and honor and power and might be to our God forever and ever! Amen." In the new creation, believers will worship God continually (7:15; cf. 11:16). The fundamental duty of human beings is to give glory to God (11:13; 14:7), and when people glorify

God, they give him thanks (11:17). The imagery of playing harps and singing a new song expresses the joy that will envelop the lives of believers in the heavenly Zion (14:1–3). Twice John is so overcome by the beauty of the angel giving him the revelation that he falls down to worship him. In both instances, John is reproved since the angel is a "fellow servant" (19:10; 22:9). The angel says, "Worship God."

In some ways, these two words summarize the message of the book of Revelation because the readers are tempted to worship the beast and Babylon, comfort and wealth, security and safety. Bauckham remarks, "It is worth noticing how far from anthropocentric is this vision of worship. Humanity is radically displaced from the centre of things where human beings naturally tend to place themselves."[8] Revelation takes us back to the first commandment (Ex. 20:3), which summons all human beings everywhere to put God first in their lives, to give him all their worship, praise, and adoration. The suffering church needs a fresh vision of God as the sovereign Creator, as the one who is awesomely beautiful and terrifying (in the good sense of the word) in his holiness. Believers are to be filled with praise and thanks, as they give all glory, honor, and worship to him, while at the same time resisting the blandishments of the beast and false prophet.

God's Judgment

The holiness of God, his absolute goodness, means that he can't tolerate evil, and thus one of the major themes of Revelation is the judgment of evil. We should note from the outset that the words about judgment are not written *to unbelievers*; they are written *for believers*, and thus they are not vengeful words hurled at unbelievers. They remind suffering believers that God is just, that everything will be set right in the end, that evil will not triumph. The judgments of God in the book, then, function to encourage believers to persevere in faith and goodness.

8   Bauckham, *Theology of Revelation*, 33.

We begin our study of judgment by considering the seal (Rev. 6:1–17; 8:1–5), trumpet (8:1–9:21; 11:15–19), and bowl judgments (16:1–21). They come in a series of three sevens, and the number seven signifies the completeness of the judgments, indicating that the judgments vindicate God's righteousness. Some maintain that these judgments refer to events prior to the destruction of Jerusalem in AD 70. Dispensationalists argue that they refer to judgments that occur in the last seven years in history. Others think that the seals, trumpets, and bowls represent the judgments that encompass all history from the ascension of Christ to his second coming. I would tweak this last view a bit and argue that the seals and trumpets represent judgments throughout history, while the bowl judgments refer to the judgments unleashed near or at the second coming. The notion that the judgments relate to the judgment on Israel before AD 70 depends on an early date for the book, which is less likely than the later date. Furthermore, there is no clear evidence in these chapters that the judgments are restricted to the land of Israel. Indeed, the opening of the sixth seal most naturally refers to judgment on the entire world, as we shall see. Also, judgment on Israel is disconnected from the life of believers in Asia Minor, most of whom were Gentiles. The dispensational view is unconvincing since there is no indication that these judgments take place after the rapture, which Revelation never mentions. Nor is there any indication that these judgments are restricted to the end of history since the events described characterize all history, in that wars, famines, plagues, and opposition to the gospel are perennial.

Seal Judgments

The seals, then, describe judgments occurring from the resurrection and ascension of Jesus to his second coming. In fact, these judgments reflect what Jesus predicted in his eschatological discourse (Matt. 24; Mark 13; Luke 21), and I will note the parallels with this discourse as we consider each of the judgments. Perhaps it will be helpful at this point to introduce a table rehearsing the seal judgments (see table 3.1).

Table 3.1   Seal Judgments

Seals	Revelation	Vision	Meaning
Seal 1	6:1–2	White horse	The Lamb's victory
Seal 2	6:3–4	Red horse	War
Seal 3	6:5–6	Black horse	Famine
Seal 4	6:7–8	Pale horse	Rampant death
Seal 5	6:9–11	The souls of the martyrs	Cry for justice and call for patience
Seal 6	6:12–17	The final earthquake	Present creation comes to an end
Seal 7	8:1–5	Silence in heaven / beginning of seven trumpets	Further judgments

These visions appropriate the Synoptic tradition about the end but express it in a fresh way. I am not arguing that Jesus's eschatological discourse should be equated with the seals in Revelation, for Jesus focuses on the judgment that will take place in Jerusalem, which culminates in the destruction of the city and the temple in AD 70. John, by way of contrast, does not discuss the judgment of Jerusalem but focuses on the judgment of the entire world. I would suggest that even in Jesus's eschatological discourse, there is a typological relationship between the judgment on Jerusalem and the final judgment. As the seal judgments in Revelation anticipate and point to the end of history (though they are not the end of history themselves), so the predictions given in Jesus's eschatological discourse anticipate the judgment of Jerusalem in AD 70, and the judgment of Jerusalem in turn points to the final judgment. We see the same phenomenon in the Old Testament, which speaks of many days of the Lord; such days of the Lord point to and anticipate the final day of the Lord.

Many different strands of tradition coalesce in the breaking of the seals. The first four seals, in which different horses emerge, evoke the horses in Zechariah 1:8–17 (cf. Zech. 6:1–8), which, in light of the entire vision in Zechariah, signify the judgment on the

nations that have oppressed Jerusalem. Similarly, the seal judgments
focus on the judgment inflicted on those who oppose the people of
God and on the coming kingdom of God.

When the first seal is broken, a rider with a white horse emerges,
and the rider holding a bow and wearing a crown goes out to conquer (Rev. 6:1–2). Some think the rider on the white horse is the
beast as a parody of Christ riding on a white horse (19:11–12).[9]
Others think the judgment is war in general.[10] I support the minor-
ity opinion that the rider is Jesus Christ since there is no indication in context that we have a parody, such as we see with the two
beasts in chapter 13, and since we have an intertextual clue from
19:11–12 that the one riding on a white horse is Christ himself. He
conquers in this case through the proclamation of the gospel, which
overcomes opposition by being believed throughout the world. We
find the same message in Jesus's eschatological discourse, where he
says, "This gospel of the kingdom will be proclaimed throughout
the whole world as a testimony to all nations, and then the end will
come" (Matt. 24:14). The parallel in Mark says, "The gospel must
first be proclaimed to all nations" (13:10). The proclamation of the
gospel will bring salvation to those who believe, but it is also a message of judgment to those who disbelieve, as those who persecute
the church resist its witness (Luke 21:12–19). One of the marks of
the age in which we live is the mission of the church, whereby the
church takes the gospel to the ends of the earth, and many believe
the good news, but others show their rebellion against God by resisting the good news that is proclaimed.

The second broken seal brings forth a "bright red" horse, and
the rider takes "peace from the earth" so that war breaks out with
a sword (Rev. 6:3–4). Jesus also predicts "wars and rumors of wars"

9   See John F. Walvoord, *The Revelation of Jesus Christ: A Commentary* (Chicago: Moody
    Press, 1966), 127. Robert L. Thomas says the rider is "a personification of a growing
    movement or force that will be at work during this future period." *Revelation 1–7: An
    Exegetical Commentary* (Chicago: Moody Press, 1992), 422.
10 Caird, *Revelation*, 80.

(Matt. 24:6; cf. Mark 13:6; Luke 21:9) and "nation [rising] against nation, and kingdom against kingdom" (Matt. 24:7; cf. Mark 13:7; Luke 21:10). The interadvent period will be characterized by war, conflict, and murder.

The opening of the third seal leads to the summons of the third horse, which is black (Rev. 6:7–8). A denarius is a day's wage, and thus a quart of wheat for a denarius and three quarts of barley for a denarius signifies that there is barely enough food to get by. Another mark of this present evil age is famine, and Jesus predicts that there will be "famines and earthquakes in various places" (Matt. 24:7; cf. Mark 13:8; Luke 21:11).

The fourth seal is represented by "a pale horse," and the enemies are "Death" and "Hades," which portends that one-fourth of the world will be slain "with sword and with famine and with pestilence and by wild beasts of the earth" (Rev. 6:8). In many ways life goes on as usual, but disasters are liable to strike at any time, and the world is characterized by such. In his eschatological discourse, Jesus mentions "pestilences" that will come on earth (Luke 21:11).

We see in these first four seals that so-called "ordinary" events—from the preaching of the gospel to wars, famines, and plagues—represent God's work in the world and particularly his judgment on human sin. The thought is quite similar to Romans 1:18–32 in that the troubles of the world constitute God's judgment. One observing such events might conclude that such disasters are the result of fate or chance, but John unveils to the reader God's perspective on such occurrences. They represent his judgments because of human evil. We should not overread what is being said here, as if John is drawing a one-to-one correspondence between difficulties in life and human evil. John recognizes that believers may suffer economic deprivation as well since they are the object of persecution and discrimination (Rev. 2:9; 13:16–17). Believers aren't on the inside with Babylon, and thus the riches and glory of such aren't available to them. In any case, John doesn't tie the judgments here to individual cases but focuses generally on the judgments unleashed on the world because of human rebellion. Still, the events in the world are not merely "sound and fury, / Signifying nothing."[11] The judgments occurring in history are a prelude to the final judgment, an indication that all is not right with the world and that the world is not rightly related to God.

The fifth seal (6:9–11) zeroes in on the death and prayers of the martyrs, those who were slaughtered and who dwell under the altar because of their devotion to God's word and because of their witness. In voicing the words "How long?" they ask the Lord to act justly and righteously since those who have murdered them have been spared, even though they had perpetrated such great evil. The answer given is that they are to rest and wait—the day of judgment is coming, but there are others who will be put to death, just as they have been put to death. The recognition that others will be put to death, incidentally, suggests that all the martyrs throughout history are included. Jesus also predicts the slaughter of believers in his eschatological discourse: "Then they will deliver you up to tribulation and put you to death, and you will be hated by all nations for my name's sake" (Matt. 24:9; cf. Mark 13:12; Luke 21:16). The interadvent period is characterized by the advancement of the gospel, by war and famine and plagues, and by the slaughter of believers because of their devotion to Christ. We can look back over two thousand years of church history and say that these things are so, that history verifies this reading of Revelation. Furthermore, believers in many parts of the world today are being slain because of their witness for Christ. The death and resurrection of Christ does not immediately overcome evil in the world; instead, evil intensifies as the people of God are put to death for Christ's sake. At the same time, John clarifies that in all these events God is working out his purposes, that his sovereignty has not been sacrificed nor his rule annulled.

The sixth seal brings us to the end of history, to the day of judgment (Rev. 6:12–17). Some interpreters fail to see this because they think Revelation is a continuous narrative and because they do not see how

11 William Shakespeare, *Macbeth*, 5.5.26–27.

the book is recursive and recapitulatory. John brings us to the end of history repeatedly in the book, and then he starts over again. Others maintain that the end can't be in view since it is the sixth instead of the seventh seal. Certainly, the end can't occur before the opening of the seventh seal (8:1–5). But such a reading fails to see that the seventh seal is a literary device that leads to the blowing of the seven trumpets, and as I shall argue shortly, the trumpets rehearse the same period as the seals from a different perspective.

We have remarkable evidence that the sixth seal represents the final judgment. First, the word "earthquake" in every instance in the book signifies the end of history (8:5; 11:13, 19; 16:18).[12] Second, the imagery picks up the "day of the Lord" imagery, which is a common feature in the Old Testament Prophets (e.g., Isa. 13:6, 9; Joel 1:15; 2:1, 11, 31; 3:14; Amos 5:18, 20; Obad. 15; Zeph. 1:7, 14; 2:2, 3; Mal. 4:5), but here we have the climactic and final day of the Lord. All the days of the Lord in the Old Testament point to and are fulfilled in this final day of the Lord. Third, we have apocalyptic language, and the apocalyptic language symbolizes the end. The entire created world is falling apart, as the sun becomes black and the moon turns to blood (Rev. 6:12; cf. Isa. 13:10; Ezek. 32:7; Joel 2:10). Similarly, the stars in the heavens are hurled from heaven to earth, signifying that the created order is unraveling (Rev. 6:13). When the sky is rolled up like a scroll (Isa. 34:4), John is telling us that life on earth is over (Rev. 6:14). In Old Testament texts, of course, life continued, even though such imagery was used. But here the imagery of the world falling apart is brought together to describe the end of the world, the final day of the Lord. The apocalyptic judgments in the Old Testament point to the final and irreversible judgment. The world won't continue forever as it is now; mountains and islands will be displaced (6:14). We have confirmation in Revelation that the moving of islands and mountains signals the end of all things.

---

12 Cf. Richard Bauckham, "The Eschatological Earthquake in the Apocalypse of John," *NovT* 19, no. 3 (1977): 224–33.

We read in Revelation 16:20—which is the seventh trumpet judgment (16:17–21), relaying the end of history—that "every island fled away, and no mountains were to be found." The end of history, in apocalyptic language, is described as the fleeing of islands and the vanishing of mountains (cf. 20:11). Fourth, that the end is at hand is evident from the response of unbelievers. They are terrified because the judgment is coming (6:15–17; cf. 19:18), begging to be spared from the God who sits on the throne and from the Lamb's wrath. John tells us that "the great day of their wrath has come" (6:17). The day of the Lord, the final judgment, has arrived.

A brief explanation of the seventh seal should suffice (8:1–5). The silence in heaven signifies that judgment is imminent, and the antecedents in Habakkuk 2:20 and Zephaniah 1:7 bear this out. The incense and the prayers of the saints indicate that the judgment on unbelievers is the result of the saints' prayers (cf. Ps. 141:2). The prayers of the saints for vindication will be answered (Rev. 6:9–11). The prayer for God's kingdom to come and his will to be done (Matt. 6:10) is climactically and fully answered in the last judgment and the arrival of the new creation.

Excursus on Richard Bauckham's Understanding of the Seals and Judgment

Perhaps this is the place to interact with Richard Bauckham's proposal regarding the seal judgments, which has implications for how he reads judgment in the book as a whole.[a] For readers not inclined to read a more technical discussion, they can move to the next section of the book. Bauckham argues that the events that take place in the unrolling of the seals are not the contents of the sealed scroll since the contents of the scroll are revealed only when *all* the seals are broken. We discover the content of the seals, according to Bauckham, in Revelation 10, with the opening of the little scroll (Gk. *biblaridion*). The key revelation of the book is delayed, says Bauckham, until chapter 10, and the importance of this revelation is certified by John's description of the glory of the angel.[b] The seal and trumpet judgments are intended to bring people to repentance, but we see from these judgments, says Bauckham, that judgments by themselves do not bring someone to faith. The seven thunders are withdrawn (10:3–4) because judgments don't bring people to repentance. Since judgments don't induce repentance, John prophesies again (10:11), and the content of the prophecy is found in 11:1–13, which Bauckham takes to be the central message of the book.

In chapter 11, we see, according to Bauckham, that the witness and proclamation of the church bring the nations to repentance and that the willingness of believers to suffer death will lead to the conversion of the nations, showing once again that judgments alone don't bring people to repentance. The martyrs as witnesses, as those who suffer for the sake of the faith, draw people to faith. The message of the two witnesses—that is, the message of the church—is fundamentally a call to repentance and not a message of judgment. We see such repentance when the survivors of the great earthquake give glory to God (11:13). Only one-tenth are judged, and nine-tenths are saved, showing that God will have mercy on "the faithless majority."[c] John has reinterpreted the song of Moses in Revelation 15 in a way that departs from Exodus 15, for in Revelation 15:4, we see that all nations will come and worship the Lord because of his mighty acts, and thus John reinterprets the song of Moses in an optimistic manner. According to Bauckham, then, 11:13–14 and 15:2–4 reflect the same basic meaning. God has saved his suffering people for the purpose of saving even more. The seven last plagues in chapter 16 can't be the judgments described in 15:3 (according to Bauckham) because the seven bowls represent total and complete judgment. And these judgments don't cause people to fear God and to repent (11:13; 15:4) but harden them even more in their sin (16:9, 11). We must also include here the final judgment in 19:11–21, according to Bauckham, and thus we have a tension between universal judgment and the universal turning of the nations to the Lord. Both pictures, he says, point to the truth and encourage God's people to be a saving witness to the nations. This universal notion is supported by 21:3, where all the "peoples" (CSB) belong to the Lord, where the tree of life brings "healing" for "the nations" (22:2).

Bauckham's notion that we see the conversion of the nations is quite stimulating and in some respects accords with the message of the book, but the reading he proposes has problems. First, his interpretation of the opening of the scrolls is unlikely. It is possible that the scroll (Gk. *biblion*) in chapter 5 and the scroll in chapter 10 (Gk. *biblaridion*) are the same. Bauckham rightly says that diminutive forms in Koine Greek do not necessarily indicate a distinction between two words. Still, even if we should not press the diminutive form,[d] it is significant that a *different word is used* in chapter 10, and thus a *clear* literary link between the two chapters isn't forged. If John had wanted us to see the connection, it would be much easier to see it if he used the exact same word in chapter 10 (Gk. *biblion*). As Beale says, John uses the word *biblion* around twenty times, and this chapter is the only place in which he uses *biblaridion* (10:2, 9, 10). He does use the term *biblion* once in chapter 10 (10:8), but *biblaridion* is more prominent.[e] The failure to use the same term consistently suggests a distinct meaning in chapter 10.

In addition, Bauckham reads the breaking of the seven seals too literally, as if all the seals have to be broken before the scroll is read. Sigve Tonstad rightly says that "the idea that the scroll's content can be known only when the scroll is opened is too literalistic."[f] John doesn't clearly signal to readers that the content of the scrolls is delayed until chapter 10. The several chapters that separate chapters 6 and 10 make it unlikely that the content of the scrolled book is delayed until chapter 10, and thus it is more natural to see the enumerated judgments in chapters 6–7 as the content of the first six seals. We are not intended to read the picture of the scroll tied up with seven seals so rigidly.

Furthermore, Bauckham emphasizes the message of salvation in Revelation 10–11, but the wording of 10:11 calls into question Bauckham's view.[g] John is told in 10:11, "You must again prophesy about many peoples and nations and languages and kings." Admittedly, it is difficult to discern whether the Greek preposition *epi* in 10:11 means "on" or "against." Most English translations leave the matter open by translating the word as "about" (CSB, ESV, NET, NIV, NLT, NRSV, RSV) or "concerning" (NASB). Some commentators argue that the preposition means "against,"[h] which calls into question Bauckham's view. The expression is used twenty-five times in the Old Testament, and Osborne says that we should translate it "prophesy about" and that the term could have both positive and negative connotations.[i] Tabb points out that the expression may point to judgment (cf. Ezek. 4:7; 6:2; 11:4; 13:2, 17; 21:2; 25:2; 28:21; 29:2) or may promise deliverance (Ezek. 36:1, 6; 37:4, 9).[j] Still, the inclusion of kings in the list ("many peoples and nations and languages and kings," 10:11) suggests a negative sense in this context since kings are typically portrayed negatively in Revelation (6:15; 16:12, 14, 16; 17:2, 9, 10, 18; 18:3, 9; 19:18, 19).[k] The eating of the scroll also makes John's stomach bitter (10:9–10), which almost certainly designates judgment, and this fits with Ezekiel, where the prophet eats the scroll given to him that has "written on it words of lamentation and mourning and woe" (Ezek. 2:10). The scroll in both Revelation 10 and Ezekiel focuses on judgment. The emphasis on judgment introduces a significant problem for Bauckham because Revelation 10 doesn't support his claim that the scroll here represents the salvation instead of the judgment of the nations.

The context of Revelation 11 also speaks against Bauckham's reading, for although the two witnesses, who represent the church, call on people to repent, the text actually emphasizes judgment rather than salvation.[l] The fire coming out of the two witnesses' mouths clearly symbolizes judgment (11:5), as does the shutting up of the sky and the striking of the earth with plagues (11:6). John appropriates the language of the Egyptian plagues and the famine that desolated Israel in Elijah's day to symbolize judgment. The opposition of the world to the church takes center stage, as the beast puts to death the witnesses (i.e., he persecutes the church), and unbelievers don't honor believers in their death by giving them a proper burial (11:7–9). Instead, they celebrate and party over the death of those belonging to God (11:10).[m] God vindicates his own by raising them from the dead and exalting them to heaven, which strikes fear in unbelievers (11:11–12).

Everything in the text of the chapter up to 11:13, then, emphasizes opposition from the world, God's vindication of his own, and the judgment of the wicked. The "great earthquake" symbolizes judgment, and the death of seven thousand signifies the destruction of the wicked (cf. Ezek. 38:19). G. K. Beale and Eckhard Schnabel provide a detailed discussion of these verses, defending the notion that judgment is intended.[n] That seven thousand are judged is doubtless symbolic, and the number may represent God's compensatory justice in contrast to the seven thousand who constitute the remnant in 1 Kings 19:18

in Israel during the time of Elijah. The judgment of a tenth points to an inaugurated judgment. Scholars dispute whether fear and giving God glory refers to believers or unbelievers, and good evidence can be adduced on both sides. Even if salvation is intended, it isn't clear, against Bauckham, that the suffering of the martyrs leads people to faith. Instead, if John refers to salvation, which I think is more likely, it is God's judgment that frightens people and leads them to glorify God. It follows, then, that if John speaks of salvation, it isn't the suffering witness of the martyrs that leads to salvation but the reality of judgment.[o]

It is also the case that the nations and peoples are saved in Revelation 15:3–4; 21:3; and 22:2. The interpretation of 15:3–4 is disputed, and some think it refers to judgment, but it seems more likely that salvation is in view since the nations fear and glorify God's name and worship him. In Revelation we have instances in which the nations refuse to repent and are judged and also cases in which they turn to God and are saved. We can't privilege one set of statements, as Bauckham does, and he comes close to endorsing universal salvation, though he qualifies his view in a footnote.[p] Furthermore, we have no clear indication of the sequential pattern drawn by Bauckham, as if there are one set of believers who are martyrs and another set drawn to faith through the suffering of the martyrs. This pattern is nowhere clearly taught in the book. Instead, John teaches consistently that some repent and believe, while others harden their hearts, refuse to repent, and are judged. So even if 15:3–4 refers to salvation, it isn't clear that the suffering of the martyrs led the "nations" to faith, as if they are two distinct groups.

a   Richard Bauckham, *Climax of Prophecy: Studies on the Book of Revelation* (London: T&T Clark, 1993), 238–337. For a short summary, see Bauckham, *Theology of Revelation*, 80–88, 98–104.

b   So also Koester, *Revelation*, 405.

c   Bauckham, *Theology of Revelation*, 87.

d   But see here Beale, *Revelation*, 531.

e   Beale, *Revelation*, 531.

f   Sigve K. Tonstad, *Revelation*, PCNT (Grand Rapids, MI: Baker Academic, 2019), 119.

g   For a more extended critique, see Eckhard J. Schnabel, "John and the Future of the Nations," *BBR* 12, no. 2 (2002): 243–71.

h   See Beale, *Revelation*, 554–55; Schnabel, "Future of the Nations," 251–53.

i   See Osborne, *Revelation*, 405.

j   Brian J. Tabb, *All Things New: Revelation as Canonical Capstone*, NSBT 48 (Downers Grove, IL: IVP Academic, 2019), 128.

k   The only exception is Rev. 21:24.

l   Cf. Schnabel, "Future of the Nations," 248–50; Beale, *Revelation*, 531.

m   See also Tabb, *All Things New*, 128.

n   Beale, *Revelation*, 602–8; Schnabel, "Future of the Nations," 250–56. For the contrary view, see Osborne, *Revelation*, 433–35.

o   Incidentally, the reality that judgments occur elsewhere (Rev. 9:20–21; 16:9, 11) doesn't eliminate this view. In the latter two passages, John isn't teaching that God's judgments *never* lead to repentance.

p   But see Mathias Rissi, who argues for universal salvation. *The Future of the World: An Exegetical Study of Revelation 19.11–22.15*, SBT, 2nd ser., vol. 23 (Naperville, IL: A. R. Allenson, 1966), 80–83.

Trumpet Judgments

The seventh seal judgment leads us to the seven trumpet judgments, which are harder to interpret than the seal judgments since the language is highly symbolic, making it difficult to discern the referents of the judgments. We wish that John inserted some commentary here to explain the referents for this imagery. There are, though, many allusions in the trumpet judgments to the plagues descending on Egypt at the exodus. I will argue that these judgments signify events that take place between the resurrection and ascension of Christ and the second coming. We have no indication in the text that these events are restricted to the judgment of Jerusalem in AD 70, nor is it clear that they refer only to the end of history. Before examining these judgments, a table listing out the trumpet judgments should prove helpful (see table 3.2).

Table 3.2   Trumpet Judgments

Trumpets	Revelation	Extent or Woe	Judgment Described
Trumpet 1	8:7	One-third of earth	Hail, fire, and blood on land
Trumpet 2	8:8–9	One-third of sea	Burning mountain thrown into the sea
Trumpet 3	8:10–11	One-third of rivers and springs	A burning star falls on rivers and springs
Trumpet 4	8:12	One-third of lights in sky	Sun, moon, and stars darkened
Trumpet 5	9:1–11	First woe	Demons from the abyss
Trumpet 6	9:13–21	Second woe	Demons from the east
Trumpet 7	11:15–19	Third woe	Kingdom come

When the first trumpet is blown by an angel, there follows "hail and fire, mixed with blood, and these [are] thrown upon the earth" (Rev. 8:7). As a consequence, fire consumes a third of the earth and the trees and all the green grass. This plague reminds us of the hail in Exodus 9:23–25, though the reference to blood is distinctive. Perhaps Ezekiel 38:22 is in view as well: "With pestilence and bloodshed I will enter into judgment with him, and I will rain upon him and his hordes and the many peoples who are with him torrential rains and hailstones, fire and sulfur." John emphasizes, however, the judgment on nature, which suggests that one consequence of sin is that the world isn't as fruitful and beneficent as it should be. The judgment should not be construed too literally because here we are told that all the green grass is consumed, but we are told in Revelation 9:4 that the locusts don't harm the grass, which scarcely makes sense if there is no grass to harm!

The second trumpet (8:8–9) unleashes a burning mountain that is cast into the sea, and a third of the sea turns to blood. We again have an echo of the plague whereby the water of the Nile turns to blood (Ex. 7:20). We see that the judgment is apportioned to one-third so that a third of creatures in the sea die and a third of the ships are destroyed.

We should not take the numbers or descriptions literally; it is John's way of saying that life on earth and in the seas stands under the judgment of God, but his judgment isn't total and comprehensive.

The blowing of the third trumpet is followed by a star falling from earth to heaven, where the star may be an angel (Rev. 8:10–11). The star falls on one-third of rivers and springs so that the water is bitter (Jer. 9:15). Perhaps this is a symbol of false teaching (Jer. 23:15), but more likely it is a general way of saying that life in this world stands under God's judgments. Every arena of life is affected, both the land and seas, and the rivers and waters. Even today, the lack of clean and refreshing water leads to the spread of disease and death.

The fourth trumpet results in a third of the sun, moon, and stars being darkened (Rev. 8:12). The judgment is certainly symbolic since life on earth could not continue if the sun were darkened in such a way. The judgment echoes the plague of darkness that settled on Egypt (Ex. 10:21–23). John uses apocalyptic language to denote the devastation that affects the entire world, and no realm is exempted since the land, the seas, the rivers, and the skies are blighted.

The fifth trumpet is remarkable and not easy to interpret (Rev. 9:1–11). A star falls from heaven to earth and opens the shaft of the abyss. Smoke swirls up out of the open shaft, and then locusts that are like scorpions flood the earth. But these locusts are unlike any locusts that ever existed because they don't eat grass, plants, and trees. Instead, they sting like scorpions and torment those who don't have God's seal on their foreheads. The anguish is unspeakable, as people long to die but continue to live. The background to the text is clearly Joel 2:1–11, although the plague of locusts in Egypt should also be included (Ex. 10:12). The locusts are compared to war horses in John's vision, just as they are in Joel 2:4. These locusts differ dramatically from ordinary locusts in that they don't eat green plants or grass, they come out of the abyss, and their leader is Apollyon (probably Satan). Thus, it seems that the locusts are demonic. They are not ordinary creatures.

But what does the vision mean? Some think that John literally describes the stings unbelievers will receive at the end of history. But in a text that is so full of symbolism, it is doubtful that we should understand the account literally. Probably John reflects on the judgment of unbelievers throughout history, and his point is that their lives are a kind of living death. In other words, unbelievers find life so miserable and painful that they long to die, to end it all, to commit suicide. And yet they don't want to take the final step and terminate their lives either, and thus their lives are like a living death. We must beware of flat-footed interpretations. Clearly, some unbelievers enjoy wonderful lives and are fulfilled in many respects. John isn't trying to describe the interior life of every individual. Still, many unbelievers live lives of quiet desperation. They are reluctant to share their fears and their misery with others. Those who don't know God experience torment and grief that is inaccessible to ordinary human observation, but John apocalyptically reveals the true state of human hearts. Sometimes believers, of course, struggle with fear and depression and despair as well, but in the midst of their stresses, they have the indwelling Spirit and the power of Christ. John isn't trying to provide a comprehensive analysis of these matters. We all face discouragement in a world full of evil, and we struggle against evil in our own hearts, but Revelation reminds us that those who give themselves to the Lord will triumph.

The sixth trumpet leads to the release of the four angels at the Euphrates River (Rev. 9:13–19). Since these angels are bound, they are almost certainly demons. Beyond the Euphrates are the enemies of Rome, the feared Parthians, and it is also the limit of the promised land (Gen. 15:18; Deut. 1:7; Josh. 1:4). John sees fearsome enemies—a force of two hundred million—released. We might think this is a human army, but the description of the army leads us in another direction because the army is certainly not human. The horses don't fit any description of horses on earth since their heads are like lions' heads, and we know that "fire and smoke and sulfur" (Rev. 9:17) don't come from the mouths of horses. We also see that they are not like horses because their tails are like serpents and they inflict injury with their tails. One-third of human beings are killed by this demonic horde, but the number should not be taken literally. It depicts the judgments that characterize human life and result in death during this present evil age.

The sixth trumpet judgment is followed by a word about repentance. Those spared judgment fail to repent but continue in their idolatry, murder, sorcery, sexual sin, and stealing (9:20–21). The apocalyptic and hyperbolic nature of this statement is evident because we get the impression from what John writes here that no one ever repents, but we see elsewhere that some do repent and believe (cf. 15:3–4). John sketches a typical and common human response to God's judgments. We see from these verses as well the justice of God's judgments because people *should* repent of their evil when they see the Lord's just verdict on sin, and yet they fail to do so. Even when they see the consequences of their actions, unbelievers irrationally continue to pursue unrighteousness.

The seventh trumpet signifies the end of history, when the reign of Christ begins and God judges those who have pursued wickedness (11:15–19). We see again the recursive character of Revelation in that the history has again come to an end. What can we say about the trumpet judgments as a whole? I have argued that they represent symbolically and apocalyptically the judgments that characterize this present evil age, focusing on the physical, psychological, and spiritual torments experienced by human beings. John *reveals* that these events signify God's judgment, but that conclusion isn't evident to unbelievers. They are just as likely to interpret what is happening as the result of chance, fate, or the chaos of the world. The judgments should lead unbelievers to repentance, but they rationalize what is happening and spin out another reality. John reminds his readers—indeed, he encourages believers—that God rules over the world, that his judgments are just and right, and that those who do evil will face the consequences. Believers should not compromise with the world since the destiny of unbelievers is one that should by all means be avoided. They are called on to hear the message sounded out by the trumpets.

Bowl Judgments

God's holiness is the framework for interpreting the bowl judgments. The theme is captured in Revelation 14:7, where with judgment impending, people are instructed to fear God, give him glory, and worship him as Creator. The sea of glass in 15:2 echoes 4:6, which signifies God's majesty. The sea being "mingled with fire" probably designates judgment.[13] Others think the reference is to the Red Sea and to Israel's deliverance.[14] But the link with 4:6 is more probable, which supports a reference to judgment. Still, the saints overcome and conquer, since, as we have already seen, they are willing to sacrifice their lives for Christ's sake. They sing, therefore, of God's justice and holiness and greatness before his judgments are unleashed. We will begin with a table to survey the judgments accompanying the pouring out of the seven bowls (see table 3.3).

Table 3.3   Bowl Judgments

Bowls	Revelation	Place of Judgment	Description of Judgment
Bowl 1	16:2	Earth	Sores on those who worship the beast
Bowl 2	16:3	Sea	Seas turn to blood and death in the sea
Bowl 3	16:4–7	Rivers and springs	Rivers and springs turn to blood
Bowl 4	16:8–9	Sun	People scorched
Bowl 5	16:10–11	Throne of the beast	Plunged into darkness
Bowl 6	16:12–16	River Euphrates	Battle of Armageddon
Bowl 7	16:17–21	Air	Kingdom come

Some interpreters who are close to my reading of the seals and trumpets claim that the seven bowls represent judgments throughout all history as well.[15] The matter is difficult and vexed since virtually all agree that the language is symbolic and that it is difficult to unravel the meaning of the symbolism. The preterist reading is unlikely because there is no indication that the judgments are limited to Israel,

---

13   Koester, *Revelation*, 631; Osborne, *Revelation*, 562; David E. Aune, *Revelation 6–16*, WBC
      52B (Nashville: Thomas Nelson, 1998), 870–71.

14   Beale, *Revelation*, 789.

15   See, e.g., Beale, *Revelation*, 808–12.

Jerusalem, or the temple. The fifth bowl is poured out on the kingdom of the beast (Rev. 16:10), and we have already seen that the kingdom of the beast represents the Roman Empire, not Jerusalem. Similarly, the judgment of Babylon (16:19) almost certainly refers to Rome instead of Jerusalem. In my view, the bowl judgments, unlike those described in the seals and trumpets, are comprehensive and complete. Thus I suggest that they don't represent judgments unleashed throughout history. Instead, in apocalyptic fashion they depict judgments that will take place near or at the end of history.

It is difficult to know what the sores of the first bowl breaking out on those who worship the beast symbolize (16:1–2). In the plagues that decimated Egypt, boils broke out on people and animals (Ex. 9:10). In any case, the sores make life on earth unbearable for those who have resisted the Lord. The absolute misery that engulfs their lives functions as a prelude to the impending judgment.

We see more clearly in the second and third bowl judgments that the end of history is at hand. When the second bowl is poured into the sea, every creature in the sea dies (Rev. 16:3), not just one-third, as in the trumpet judgments (8:8–9). Similarly, the third bowl being poured out leads to all the rivers and springs turning to blood (16:4), not just one-third, as in the trumpet judgment (8:10–11). Whatever these symbols mean, such judgments must convey the end of history because life can hardly continue when the resources that sustain life are totally ruined. We have a hint that these judgments represent the end or imminence of the end because God is described here as the one "who is and who was" (16:5), and his role as the one "who is to come" is left out. We see the same omission of "who is to come" in 11:17, which virtually all interpreters agree represents the end of history, since the kingdoms of the world become "the kingdom of our Lord and of his Christ" (11:15). The reason for the omission of the Lord's coming in 16:5 is because the judgments unleashed on the world represent the culmination of history. Life on earth is ending.

The ferocity of the judgments leads to some questions. Are these judgments disproportionate, and do they represent injustice on God's part?

Is it fair and right for the Lord to unleash such suffering on the world, specifically on unbelievers? Many people ask such questions today about God's judgment, and we see from John's words that the same questions were asked when he wrote, that we are not the first to ask such questions. Understanding that the questions were asked in the past is important because we tend to think that we are more sensitive to evil and that we have a higher sense of justice than those who preceded us. In any case, in the midst of the judgments, John pauses to answer a question about God's justice (16:5–7). He emphasizes God's righteousness in judgment, indicating that his judgments are just since the world has spilled the blood of the saints. As a consequence, unbelievers are now drinking blood. We have a clear example here of retributive justice, in which the punishment fits the crime. Thus, we are told that unbelievers "deserve" (Gk. *axioi*) their punishments, that the judgments poured out on them are fitting. God shows his almighty power and justice and truth in punishing unbelievers, in inflicting his wrath on them.

When the fourth bowl is poured out, people are scorched with fire (16:8–9), and again we contrast this with the trumpet judgments, in which one-third of the light of the sun, moon, and stars is affected (8:10–11). Some understand the judgment literally, but perhaps the judgment signifies the psychological agony that the ungodly experience. John zeroes in on the fact that they did not repent when these judgments arrived, which is the same theme that concludes the trumpet judgments (9:20–21). God's judgments, which are warranted and deserved, should soften hearts, but instead those who have sided with the beast are infuriated and blaspheme his name. Their response accords with the proverb,

When a man's folly brings his way to ruin,
   his heart rages against the LORD. (Prov. 19:3)

The fifth bowl is quite similar to the fourth, but here the kingdom of the beast is engulfed in darkness, and the tongues of unbelievers are seized with pain (Rev. 16:10). The darkness harks back to the plague of darkness in Egypt (Ex. 10:22), and perhaps since this is the fifth bowl, John compares this to the dark smoke from the abyss in the fifth trumpet (Rev. 9:1–2). Nevertheless, once again unbelievers blaspheme and refuse to repent (16:11).

Just as the sixth trumpet meant the release of the terrible horde at the Euphrates (9:13–19), so in the sixth bowl, the waters of the Euphrates are dried up to prepare the way for eastern kings (16:12–16). Here demonic powers, using the beast and false prophet, induce the world to engage in one last battle, the battle of Armageddon. The reference to Armageddon is clearly symbolic since the word means "mountain of Megiddo," but Megiddo is a plain, not a mountain. Thus John signals to the reader that the great battles that took place in Megiddo in history (e.g., Judg. 5:19; 2 Kings 9:27; 23:29; cf. Zech. 12:11) will culminate in the greatest battle of all, but we should not conclude that it will take place geographically at Megiddo.[16]

The seventh bowl is clearly the end of history since we read, "It is done!" (Rev. 16:17), and the terror of the final judgment is conveyed (16:17–21). We see again the recursive nature of Revelation in that the sixth seal (6:12–17), the seventh trumpet (11:15–19), and the seventh bowl (16:17–21) refer to the final judgment. One of the functions of the judgment, as noted before, is to encourage believers to persevere. When we examine the world, it seems that justice is a mirage and is even laughable. Those who believe in final justice can be dismissed as deluded or as incredibly unsophisticated and naive. But John assures his readers that God will make everything right, that every wrong will be addressed, and that everyone who pursues goodness will be rewarded.

Judgment of Babylon

The judgment of Babylon is related in Revelation 17:1–19:6. Babylon is almost certainly Rome since it is described as "the great city that has dominion over the kings of the earth" (17:18). Some preterists think the city is Jerusalem, but this is quite unlikely since Jerusalem didn't

16 See Meredith Kline, "Har Megedon: The End of the Millennium," *JETS* 39, no. 2 (1996): 207–22. See also the discussion in Koester, *Revelation*, 660–61, 667.

exercise power over the kings of the earth but was itself subject to Rome. The fundamental reason for Rome's judgment was its spiritual prostitution (17:1, 4, 5, 15, 16; 19:2). Indeed, she is the "mother of prostitutes" (17:5), and Babylon's role as such is designated a "mystery" (17:5). A mystery indicates something hidden that is now revealed, fitting with the apocalyptic character of the book. What does John have in mind in talking about a mystery? From the beginning of biblical history, Babylon was opposed to the Lord (Gen. 10:10; 11:1–9), representing also the great enemy of Israel, the nation that destroyed the temple and sent the nation into exile. Perhaps the mystery is that Babylon, so to speak, keeps manifesting itself as history unfolds. Alternatively, Beale argues that the mystery has to do with how Babylon self-destructs by imploding from within instead of being destroyed by outside powers.[17] It seems more likely that John discloses that Rome is a modern manifestation of Babylon of old. It isn't glorious and beautiful but wicked and ugly.

The prophets regularly predict the judgment and demise of Babylon (e.g., Isa. 13:1–14:23; 21:1–9; Jer. 50:1–51:64). The spirit of ancient Babylon lives on in Rome, and so the enemy of the one true God has arisen in another form, having the same nature and character as the whore of ancient times. In the Old Testament, failure to worship the Lord is often described as harlotry (Isa. 57:3–5; Jer. 2:20; 3:1–10; 13:27; Ezek. 16:1–63; 20:30–32; 23:1–49; Hos. 1:1–3:5; 4:10–18; 5:3–4; 6:10; 9:1). The fundamental sin of Babylon is idolatry, the degodding of God. She "glorified herself," as Revelation 18:7 says, instead of giving glory, honor, and praise to the one true God. The kings, merchants, and sailors of the earth have climbed into bed with Babylon (17:2; 18:3, 9–24), for they have lived for the luxury, riches, status, and comfort that come from being aligned with Babylon.

The final judgment of Babylon is portrayed, and the mourning of kings, merchants, and sailors is a literary device. It is not as if they are spared from the judgment themselves! John communicates the grief and desolation experienced by those who see the entire world they

17 Beale, *Revelation*, 858.

worshiped and adored imploding. The day of their riches and wealth has come to an end—never again will they enjoy the joys of this world (18:11–19). No more entrancing and beautiful music, no more technological wizardry, no more dazzling lights from the city, no more lovely weddings (18:22–23). We also see the symbiotic relationship between Rome as the capital of the empire and the beast. The woman sits on the beast (17:3), indicating that the beast supports the capital. Still, as Paul says in Romans, God hands people over to evil (Rom. 1:24, 26, 28), and evil is inherently self-destructive and finally implodes on itself. The beast and its kings will turn against the harlot and will burn her with fire (Rev. 17:16). Evil carries within itself, by God's design, the seeds of its own destruction so that it unravels from within. God's purposes and intentions are carried out in the implosion of evil (17:17), showing God's sovereign rule over evil. In the midst of evil, God is working out his purposes, although God himself is not besmirched by sin.

The punishment meted out to the harlot is warranted since Rome has lived with luxury but drinks the blood of those devoted to Jesus (17:4–6; 18:24). Those who side with the beast are actually fighting against the Lamb, but their opposition is futile (17:14). Ultimately, the city of man, which is symbolized by Rome, will be utterly desolate and forsaken, barren and bleak as "a dwelling place for demons" and "a haunt for every unclean and detestable beast" (18:2). Rome thought she would be queen, not just for a day but forever, and that she would never experience grief and sorrow (18:7). It may look as if God has forgotten what Babylon has done and doesn't recall its sins, but the day of remembrance is coming (18:4), and then Babylon will be paid back for what it has done (18:4), confirming that God is just and righteous.

The message for believers is that they must not join hands with Babylon; they must "come out of her" and avoid the impending judgment (18:4). John forecasts future judgment to motivate the saints so that they refuse to compromise with Babylon and to capitulate to its charms. And when the judgment comes, how will the saints respond? With sorrow and grief and regret? They will rejoice by exclaiming, "Hallelujah!" In fact, the word "Hallelujah" is repeated four times in a short compass (19:1, 3, 4, 6). Is this a twisted response, an indication that the book of Revelation is vindictive and mean spirited and contrary to the grace and love that are in Christ Jesus? Far from it. As long as life on earth continues, all peoples are called on to repent and to worship the Lord (14:7). Believers are to pray and work for the salvation of all; they are to love their enemies and pray that they will be blessed (Matt. 5:43–47). They, like the Lord, long for all to be saved (1 Tim. 2:4) and don't delight in the death of the wicked (Ezek. 18:32). But here John describes the last day, the day when all wrongs are righted, the day when God judges all for what they have done. John zooms ahead to the day when the time for repentance has ended—the final day of judgment and salvation. And the final judgment is not vindictive but represents God's righteous and holy character, for "his judgments," as Revelation 19:2 says, "are true and just." The earth has been "corrupted" by the false and dehumanizing worship promoted by the harlot, and the Lord is justly avenging "the blood of his servants" (19:2). The judgment of the harlot shows that evil will not endure, that goodness will triumph, and that "the Lord our God / the Almighty reigns" (19:6). If we think joy over the fall of Babylon is sub-Christian, we should think of the fall of Hitler's Third Reich or the implosion of Communism in 1989, which were greeted with wild rejoicing since evil with all its terrors had come crashing down.

Images of the Final Judgment

One of the most dramatic pictures of the final judgment is Jesus's coming on a white horse (Rev. 19:11–21). We will pick up this theme in due course when we discuss the role of Jesus in Revelation. Another text in which there is terrifying imagery of judgment is 14:9–11. Those who worship the beast and its image "will drink the wine of God's wrath" (14:10). The cup represents God's anger and wrath, as it often does in the Old Testament (Pss. 11:6; 75:9; Isa. 51:17, 22; Jer. 25:15). Those who are the object of God's anger will be tormented by God in the presence of the angels and the Lamb, and "the smoke of their torment [will go] up forever and ever" (Rev. 14:10–11; see Isa. 34:10).

The imagery might suggest annihilation at first glance, but the smoke, which is everlasting, stems from their torment, indicating that the torment doesn't cease.[18] It is quite strained to say that the smoke continues forever if the suffering isn't everlasting. The ongoing or eternal nature of punishment is confirmed by the next line, for those who worship the beast will have "no rest, day or night" (Rev. 14:11), showing that their anguish is unending.

Another riveting image of the final judgment is depicted with God seated on "a great white throne" (20:11). The final judgment is certainly in view since earth and heaven flee and are no longer found (20:11), which is a colorful way of saying that the present created order has come to an end (6:14; 21:1), that the final day has come. If we had any doubts about it being the last day, our qualms are dispelled when all the dead are standing before the throne, and books are opened (20:12). The dead are judged by their works, and if the requisite works were done, their names are inscribed in the book of life (20:12–15). The necessity of good works to receive a final reward is confirmed in three other texts near the end of the book (21:8; 22:12, 15). Despite the claims of some, there is no evidence that the judgment described here is limited to unbelievers, since as we see in 21:8; 22:12; and 22:15, all without exception are judged according to their works.

The emphasis on judgment in Revelation may strike us as a theme that is alien to the rest of the New Testament, where salvation and God's love seem more prominent. Some might dismiss the book as a regression to a God of wrath, which the New Testament witness allegedly left behind. Still, Revelation reaffirms that a Marcionite reading of the Old Testament neglects both the Old Testament and the revelation of the true God in the New Testament. Judgment and justice reflect God's holiness, which is fundamental to God's character. Elevating God's love over his holiness distorts the nature of love since love and holiness are not opposed to one another but together play an integral part in God's

---

18 See Osborne, *Revelation*, 541–42. Koester says, "The most direct reading of the text, however, is that it pictures torment without end." *Revelation*, 614.

character. Furthermore, a right reading of the rest of the New Testament indicates that God's justice is not left behind.

The pastoral dimension in the emphasis on justice must not be neglected. The theme may seem alien when the church prospers and is celebrated in society. But when Christians face discrimination, hatred, persecution, and martyrdom, when believers see agonizing suffering in the real world (which are not just words on a page), they wonder if faithfulness to Christ is worth it. They question whether giving oneself to evil has consequences, whether there is finally justice and righteousness in the world. If evil is perpetrated and there is no justice, evil is evacuated as a moral category. God's justice and judgment underscore that decisions in life are significant, that there is such a thing as good and evil, and that the world isn't the product of blind fate.

We are reminded in the emphasis on judgment that salvation is from the Lord (Rev. 7:10; 12:10; 19:1), for all deserve to be judged. The salvation of any is due to God's grace (1:4) and to his redeeming work (14:3–4). God's eschatological salvation is connected to the judgment of the wicked, for ultimate deliverance is realized when the wicked are judged (19:1–2), when evil is removed totally from the scene and banished to the lake of fire.

Conclusion

The readers of Revelation need to hear the truth about who God is and what he does. He is sovereign and holy, and therefore he judges sin as Almighty God, as the Holy One of Israel. The church needs to hear this message because the sovereignty of God reminds them in their suffering that the world isn't spinning out of God's control; it still resides within the orbit of God's sovereignty. In the midst of suffering, believers may wonder if God is good, if he has forgotten them. But if they open their ears, they will hear the truth. God is infinitely holy, and his holiness can't tolerate sin. Thus believers can be comforted that God will judge the world. They are comforted by God's judgment not because they take glee in seeing their enemies punished; they are comforted because they are reminded that evil will not triumph, that goodness will have the final say and will be the final reality.

The Good News of the Lion and the Lamb

THE READERS OF REVELATION need to hear about opponents so that they are aware of the challenges they face, which include the dragon, the two beasts, and Babylon. In the midst of such suffering and despite their adversaries, the believers need to have ears to hear and must persevere until the end and refuse to compromise so that they will experience eschatological blessing. Still, they need ammunition to endure, and John reminds them of God's sovereignty, holiness, and judgment. Endurance will be rewarded because evil doesn't rule history. God is still the ruler of all, and as the Holy One, he will not tolerate evil.

At the same time—and this is the subject of the present chapter—the readers need to be reminded of the message about Jesus Christ. One should not be surprised that the chapter on Jesus is the longest in this book since he is the center of Revelation. He is the Messiah, the King of Israel, and the descendant of David, but at the same time, he is fully divine, sharing equally in the divine nature with the Father. As the Son of David and the Son of God, Jesus has redeemed and freed his people from their sins. Believers are spared from the judgment ultimately because of the grace of Christ granted to them through his death. The evil in their lives has been washed away by the blood of the Lamb, and thus they are able to dwell joyfully in God's presence forever. Jesus will come again and bring in his kingdom, judging those who oppose him and rewarding his own.

The Identity of Jesus

One of the striking features of Revelation, one that actually suggests that the apostle John is the author (assuming here that the Gospel was written by the apostle), is its extraordinarily high Christology. We begin by documenting the numerous places where Jesus and God share the same status, and these texts are truly quite astonishing.

The first example is located in the grace wish, which is a typical feature in the opening of New Testament letters (Rev. 1:4–6). What stands out is that grace and peace come not only from the God of Exodus 3:14 (see Rev. 1:4) but also from Jesus Christ (1:5). Here we limit ourselves to noting that he is designated "the ruler of kings on earth" and that he has "made us a kingdom, priests to his God and Father" (1:5). Two observations should be made. First, only God rules over kings; such a thing is never said of human beings. The pastoral impact of these words is also significant since a suffering church, a church in which some believers were losing their lives, would be tempted to doubt whether God rules. John teaches them that Christ rules over every king, and thus no earthly power has ultimate sovereignty. Second, in the same way, only God has the right to constitute people as a kingdom and his priests (1:6). Yahweh appointed Israel to be "a kingdom of priests" when he established the covenant with them at Sinai (Ex. 19:6; cf. Isa. 61:6). Attributing such a function to Jesus Christ, then, is quite remarkable, showing that he has the same stature and identity as Yahweh.

We also find in Revelation 1 a visionary appearance of Jesus as the Son of Man (1:12–18), where John clearly draws on the "son of man" tradition in Daniel 7:13–14. A reference to the Son of Man is unexpected since outside the Gospels we find a reference to the Son of Man only in Acts 7:56. We also have several pieces of evidence here that the Son of Man has the same stature and identity as God himself. We are told that the Son of Man has hair "like white wool, like snow" (Rev. 1:14). At first glance this might seem unexceptional, but when we travel back to Daniel 7:9, Yahweh has "clothing . . . white as snow" and "hair . . . like pure wool." John hasn't clumsily merged together two distinct texts in the Old Testament. In his allusions to the Old Testament, he often tweaks and readjusts the source text, and he does so to make a theological point. Here the white hair on the Son of Man indicates that he is eternal and wise just as Yahweh is eternal and wise, that he has the same identity and status as Yahweh.[1]

The Son of Man's eyes are "like a flame of fire" (Rev. 1:14), and we find the same statement repeated on two more occasions in Revelation. Even though a similar expression is used to describe an angel whose "eyes" are "like flaming torches" in Daniel (Dan. 10:6), the nature of Jesus's knowledge and the context of the entire vision in Revelation indicate divine omniscience. We find a reference to Jesus's penetrating eyes also in the letter to the church in Thyatira (Rev. 2:18), where the church tolerates the prophecies and teaching of Jezebel (2:18–29). Jesus discerns and knows the nefarious teaching propagated in Thyatira; nothing is hidden from him. We see the same theme as well in 19:12, where Jesus comes on a white horse with eyes of fiery flame to judge unbelievers, showing that his judgment is just and based on the facts. He has an exhaustive and comprehensive knowledge of those whom he will judge. Jesus's extraordinary knowledge is emphasized repeatedly in the letters to the churches: seven times he says about the state of the churches, "I know" (2:2, 9, 13, 19; 3:1, 8, 15). The seven occurrences of "I know" are not accidental; they signify the perfect and infinite knowledge of the Son of Man, showing that he knows all reality exhaustively, just as God knows all things completely.

In reading that the voice of Jesus is "like the roar of many waters" (1:15), it is difficult to know the precise significance. Ezekiel 1:24 records that the wings of the cherubim sound like many waters as well, and thus

1   See David E. Aune, *Revelation 6–16*, WBC 52B (Nashville: Thomas Nelson, 1998), 94–95; G. K. Beale, *The Book of Revelation: A Commentary on the Greek Text*, NIGTC (Grand Rapids, MI: Eerdmans, 1999), 209; Grant R. Osborne, *Revelation*, BECNT (Grand Rapids, MI: Baker Academic, 2002), 90; Otfried Hofius, *Neutestamentliche Studien*, WUNT 132 (Tübingen: Mohr Siebeck, 2000), 226.

the sound doesn't necessarily signify deity. But even there we are told that the cherubim have a voice like the Almighty. The same sound is later described as harpists strumming their harps (Rev. 14:2), and we hear the loud praise of the multitude when Babylon is judged (19:6). The point is probably that Jesus speaks with the same strength as God, for as Ezekiel relates in Ezekiel 43:2, "The glory of the God of Israel was coming from the east. And the sound of his coming was like the sound of many waters, and the earth shone with his glory." The roar of Jesus's voice points to the glory, majesty, and splendor that he shares with the Lord.

Jesus's deity is also suggested by his holding seven stars (Rev. 1:16, 20; 2:1; 3:1), since the stars are angels, indicating Jesus's sovereignty over angels, which suggests divine authority. Given everything else we have seen, that Jesus's face is "like the sun shining in full strength" (1:16) points to his divine identity. The expression in and of itself doesn't signify Jesus's divine nature since an angel's face shines like the sun as well (Dan. 10:6; Rev. 10:1). Still, the immediate context is decisive in interpreting the meaning of the vision. John faints at seeing the Son of Man in his splendor and unrivaled beauty (1:17). Jesus places his hands on him, tells him not to fear, and then proclaims, "I am the first and the last" (1:17), which is also reaffirmed in the message to the church at Smyrna (2:8) and near the end of the book (22:13). The divine identity of the Son of Man could not be clearer, for Yahweh says in Isaiah 44:6,

> I am the first and I am the last;
>> besides me there is no god.

We find a similar claim about Yahweh in Isaiah 48:12.[2] It isn't far fetched to say that John knew Isaiah well since Revelation is permeated with Old Testament allusions. No Old Testament book emphasizes the oneness and exclusivity of Yahweh more than Isaiah. Apparently, John believes the Son of Man shares the same status, identity, and nature as Yahweh

---

2   Cf. Richard Bauckham, *The Theology of the Book of Revelation*, New Testament Theology (Cambridge: Cambridge University Press, 1993), 55.

without compromising the oneness of God. As Richard Bauckham says, John "does not designate him a second god, but includes him in the eternal being of the one God of Israel who is the only source and goal of all things."[3]

Another fascinating piece of evidence is closely related to the claim that Jesus is the first and the last. Twice God is described as "the Alpha and the Omega" (Rev. 1:8; 21:6), and the latter occurrence of this phrase (21:6) immediately adds the words "the beginning and the end." Similarly, Jesus declares, "I am the Alpha and the Omega, the first and the last, the beginning and the end" (22:13). Just as God is the Alpha and the Omega and the beginning and the end, so is Jesus. Nothing could be clearer: Jesus is divine, just as the Father is divine. This fits remarkably well with the beginning of John's Gospel: "In the beginning was the Word, and the Word was with God, and the Word was God" (John 1:1). Jesus shares the same identity with God eternally.

The high Christology in Revelation could be called into question by Revelation 3:14, where Jesus is identified as "the beginning [Gk. $arch\bar{e}$] of God's creation." One could read this as if Jesus were the first creature created, which would fit with an Arian interpretation. But the incredibly high Christology of Revelation makes this reading impossible.[4] Instead, John may be designating Jesus as "the originator of God's creation" (CSB), that is, in terms of physical creation. We see similar conceptions of Jesus's role in creation in Colossians 1:15–17 and 1 Corinthians 8:6.[5] Or perhaps the emphasis is on Jesus's rule over all creation.[6] Alternatively, John may be suggesting that Jesus is the beginning and founder of the new creation, and if this is the sense, perhaps John is thinking of his resurrection from the dead.[7] In any case, there is no room for saying

---

3   Bauckham, *Theology of Revelation*, 58.
4   See the discussion in Brian J. Tabb, *All Things New: Revelation as Canonical Capstone*, NSBT 48 (Downers Grove, IL: IVP Academic, 2019), 62–63.
5   So Hofius, *Neutestamentliche Studien*, 230n42; Osborne, *Revelation*, 204–5; Bauckham, *Theology of Revelation*, 56.
6   Craig R. Koester, *Revelation: A New Translation with Introduction and Commentary*, AB 38A (New Haven, CT: Yale University Press, 2014), 336.
7   Cf. Beale, *Revelation*, 298.

that Jesus is a created being, for such a conclusion would contradict the overwhelming evidence for his deity in the book.

We also discover fascinating convergences in which God and Jesus are given the same status, and John draws these parallels repeatedly. We have seen that the four living creatures give "glory and honor and thanks" to God, who sits on the throne (Rev. 4:9), and the twenty-four elders exclaim that God is "worthy . . . to receive glory and honor and power" (4:11). But in chapter 5, the four living creatures and twenty-four elders prostrate themselves before the Lamb (5:8), singing that he is "worthy" (Gk. *axios*, 5:9), and then they are joined by countless angels proclaiming that the Lamb is "worthy"

> to receive power and wealth and wisdom and might
> and honor and glory and blessing! (5:12)

The Lamb is said to be worthy just as God is worthy, and honor and glory are given to both.[8] Indeed, all creatures exclaim,

> To him who sits on the throne and to the Lamb
> be blessing and honor and glory and might forever and ever! (5:13)

Then the four living creatures add their "Amen" as the twenty-four elders fall prostrate in worship (5:14). John has removed any room for doubt: the one on the throne and the Lamb are worshiped together and equally. As Bauckham states, "John does not wish to represent Jesus as an alternative object of worship alongside God, but as one who shares in the glory due to God. He is worthy of divine worship because his worship can be included in the worship of the one God."[9] This is certainly one of the most astonishing texts in the New Testament from the hand

8   See Hofius, *Neutestamentliche Studien*, 234.
9   Bauckham, *Theology of Revelation*, 60. John "includes Jesus in the eternal being of God without stepping outside the Jewish monotheism which for him was axiomatic." Bauckham, 61. See also Richard Bauckham, *Climax of Prophecy: Studies on the Book of Revelation* (London: T&T Clark, 1993), 137.

of one who was raised and nurtured in strict monotheism. Bauckham rightly concludes that John's presentation of Christ can't be limited to function but also includes ontology.[10]

The shared role and identity of God and the Lamb continue as the book unfolds. As the day of judgment beckons, people ask to be hidden "from the face of him who is seated on the throne, and from the wrath of the Lamb" (6:16). Indeed, "the great day of their wrath has come" (6:17). The plural pronoun "their" confirms that the wrath on the great day of the Lord, the day that is often predicted by Old Testament prophets (e.g., Joel 2:11; 3:4; Zeph. 1:14), is one when the wrath of both God and the Lamb is poured out, showing that the Lamb occupies the same status as God. Similarly, those delivered from the great tribulation stand "before the throne and before the Lamb" (Rev. 7:9). They cry out, "Salvation belongs to our God who sits on the throne, and to the Lamb!" (7:10). Both final judgment and salvation are ascribed to God and the Lamb.

We see another example of the convergence of Christ and God in the seventh trumpet, which represents the end of history. The world's kingdoms become "the kingdom of our Lord and of his Christ," and it is said that "he shall reign forever and ever" (11:15). But then 11:17 says that Almighty God has "taken [his] great power / and [has] begun to reign." It seems fair to conclude that both God and Christ reign equally for all eternity. We see a similar theme in the account of Satan's downfall, although in this instance the rule of God and Christ represents the reign that begins at the cross, and thus the text doesn't zero in on the culmination of history: "Now the salvation and the power and the kingdom of our God and the authority of his Christ have come" (12:10). Here again both salvation and kingdom authority are predicated equally of both God and his Christ, although here the reference to Jesus as the Christ may focus on his messianic reign as the Davidic descendant.

In 14:1–5, the redeemed—the 144,000—are on Mount Zion, which represents the heavenly Jerusalem (21:1). They belong to the Lamb and God since the Lamb's name and the name of the Father are inscribed

10 Bauckham, *Theology of Revelation*, 63.

on their foreheads (14:1). The equality of the Lamb and the Father surfaces again in 14:4, where the redeemed are said to be "firstfruits for God and the Lamb." The convergences continue, for there is a song of Moses and of the Lamb (15:3), and yet the song praises not the Lamb but the "Lord God the Almighty," who is "King of the nations" (15:3). All will "fear" and "glorify" and worship his great name since he is the only one who is holy (15:4). Some might think the relationship between the Lamb and God should not be pressed here, but John regularly puts the Lamb on the same level as God. What we find here is that the redemption accomplished by the Lamb is adumbrated in advance by the exodus accomplished through Moses.

Jesus is also identified as "Lord of lords and King of kings" (17:14; cf. 19:16). In the Old Testament, pagan kings are identified as "king of kings" (Ezra 7:12; Ezek. 26:7; Dan. 2:37), but only Yahweh is said to be "Lord of lords" (Deut. 10:17; Ps. 136:3). Remarkably, Jesus as the Lamb is also identified as the shepherd of the people of God (Rev. 7:17), and we are reminded of the Gospel of John, where Jesus says that he is the good shepherd (John 10:11, 14). In the Old Testament, Yahweh is the shepherd of his people (Pss. 23:1; 28:9; 80:1; Isa. 40:11; Ezek. 34:12, 15; Mic. 7:14), and the claim that Jesus is the shepherd in Revelation suggests his deity, though there are also texts in which the shepherd is Davidic (Ezek. 34:23; 37:24; Mic. 5:4), and perhaps both themes are present here.[11]

John is so amazed by the glory of the angel who interacts with him that he worships the angel by prostrating himself before him, but the angel reproves John, instructing him to worship God alone (Rev. 19:10). At the same time, the uniqueness of Jesus stands out since fellow believers adhere "to the testimony of Jesus" so that Jesus stands apart from both angels and human beings (19:10). Furthermore, we find the mysterious saying "The testimony of Jesus is the spirit of prophecy" (19:10). We don't have space to unpack and discuss the meaning of this elusive statement in detail. Robert Mounce says that "the message

11 On this matter, see Osborne, *Revelation*, 331–32; Beale, *Revelation*, 442–43.

attested by Jesus is the essence of prophetic proclamation."[12] Beale
suggests that prophetic spirits testify to Jesus.[13] Probably John means
that Spirit-inspired prophecy centers on the majesty and greatness of
Jesus,[14] and this in a verse that stresses that worship should be restricted
to God alone; thus, John exalts Jesus Christ, implying that he has the
same stature as God. In any case, the worship given to Jesus Christ in
chapter 5 shows that he is distinct from and superior to angels, and
that he deserves the same worship as God. John does not believe that
the worship of Jesus compromises monotheism, and thus the worship
of Jesus does not constitute the worship of a second god.

Those who triumph over the second death and reign for a thousand
years are also designated "priests of God and of Christ" (20:6), and the
equality of God and Christ is implied by putting them together. As the
book comes to an end, we have a flurry of references in which God and
the Lamb are placed together. For instance, there is no temple in the
heavenly Jerusalem, "for its temple is the Lord God the Almighty and
the Lamb" (21:22). Similarly, the sun and moon no longer illuminate
the city, "for the glory of God gives it light, and its lamp is the Lamb"
(21:23). The river from the city flows "from the throne of God and of
the Lamb" (22:1), and again in 22:3, John reaffirms that "the throne of
God and of the Lamb will be in it [the city]."

John doesn't merely affirm that Jesus shares the same identity and
status as God; he reaffirms this notion frequently, and thus we can
say with confidence that John in Revelation communicates one of the
highest Christologies in the entire New Testament. Interestingly, John
doesn't linger in Revelation over Jesus's titles, though he is identified as
"the Son of God" (2:18), "the son of man" (1:13; 14:14), "The Word of
God" (19:13), "Christ" (1:1, 2, 5; 11:15; 12:10; 20:4, 6), and "Lord" (11:8,
15; 14:13; 17:14; 19:16; 22:20, 21). John shows us in myriad ways that

12   Robert H. Mounce, *The Book of Revelation*, NICNT (Grand Rapids, MI: Eerdmans, 1977),
     342. So also George Eldon Ladd, *A Commentary on the Revelation of John* (Grand Rapids,
     MI: Eerdmans, 1972), 251.
13   Beale, *Revelation*, 947–48.
14   See Bauckham, *Theology of Revelation*, 161.

Jesus is fully divine. As the Son of God, Jesus has a unique relationship with the Father.[15] When we compare these titles with John's Gospel, they stand out for their relative infrequency in Revelation, although the convergence between John's Gospel regarding Jesus being the "Word" (John 1:1, 14) is striking. Even in this instance, however, the context in which the term is used is quite different.

The lordship of Jesus and his messianic status also stand out in John's vision. The prophecies about a Davidic Messiah have been fulfilled in Jesus, and it is instructive that at the outset of the book, Jesus's messianic role is stated three times (Rev. 1:1, 2, 5).[16] Elsewhere, his messiahship is associated with the culmination of history (11:15), the defeat of Satan (12:10), and the rule of saints with Christ (20:4, 6). The promises made in the covenant with David (2 Sam. 7; Ps. 89) find their fulfillment in Jesus. When we examine the places where Jesus is called Messiah and Lord, the emphasis is on his triumph, which is not surprising since Revelation emphasizes God's victory over evil through Christ. John also calls attention to Jesus's messianic role by calling him "the Lion of the tribe of Judah" (Rev. 5:5). John picks up here the word about Judah being a lion in Genesis 49:9, where the theme is Judah's preeminence and triumph over all foes.[17] Certainly, his royal majesty, strength, dignity, and beauty are communicated in Revelation as well with the word "Lion." He is also said to be "the Root of David" (Rev. 5:5) and "the root and the descendant of David" (22:16). As David's offspring, he is qualified to be the Messiah, and the term "root" (Gk. *rhiza*) harks back to Isaiah 11:1:

> There shall come forth a shoot from the stump [Gk. *rhizēs*] of Jesse,
>   and a branch from his roots [Gk. *rhizēs*] shall bear fruit.

In the Septuagint the word "stump" and the plural "roots" are both from the singular term "root" (Gk. *rhiza*). Some might think that we

---

15   See Osborne, *Revelation*, 153.
16   Cf. Bauckham, *Theology of Revelation*, 68–69.
17   There may also be an allusion to Num. 23:24 and 24:9. See Beale, *Revelation*, 349; Osborne, *Revelation*, 253.

don't have an allusion to Isaiah 11:1 (cf. Isa. 11:10) since Isaiah speaks of a root of Jesse and John of the root of David. But it is just like John to tweak the Old Testament antecedent, and thus we have another indication of the fulfillment of messianic prophecy.

In Revelation the significance of Jesus isn't communicated primarily through titles, although the titles also confirm his stature. Virtually every title predicated of Jesus in the Gospel of John is reaffirmed in Revelation, and there is no need to rehearse their significance again. Instead, the greatness and majesty of Jesus is emphasized in a distinctive and striking fashion that accords with the titles that pervade the Gospel of John. What is clear is that Jesus shares the same stature and identity as God without compromising or denying monotheism, and thus Revelation contributes significantly to the Christology that led the church to a Trinitarian conception of God.

The Lamb and Salvation

We have seen the remarkably high Christology of Revelation. The book also emphasizes the saving work of Christ, and in doing so, it echoes one of the major themes of the New Testament, showing that Revelation fits with the mainstream message of the New Testament. We have just discussed the person of Jesus in the previous section, but here we turn our attention to what he has accomplished, to his saving work. An interesting place to begin is Jesus's role as the Son of Man who harvests the earth (Rev. 14:14–16). David Aune thinks the reference here is to an angel,[18] but the title Son of Man points to Jesus Christ rather than an angelic figure.[19] The use of the same phrase in the book should take hermeneutical precedence (cf. 1:12–16) and points us to how "son of man" should be understood in 14:14. Earlier in the book, Jesus comes "with the clouds" (1:7), and thus the one sitting on the cloud is Jesus.[20]

---

18 Aune, *Revelation 6–16*, 840–42.
19 So G. B. Caird, *A Commentary on the Revelation of St. John the Divine*, HNTC (New York: Harper & Row, 1966), 190–91; Mounce, *Revelation*, 279; Beale, *Revelation*, 770–72; Osborne, *Revelation*, 550.
20 So Koester, *Revelation*, 622–23.

Here he is seated on a cloud, and in Isaiah 19:1 (LXX), Yahweh is seated on a cloud.[21]

Some understand the harvest here to be the final judgment since the harvest in the immediately succeeding text certainly depicts judgment (Rev. 14:17–20). The allusion to Joel 3:13 in Revelation 14:15 also leads some to the same conclusion since Joel clearly describes judgment instead of salvation.[22] Still, the arguments supporting two different harvests, one that is salvific (Rev. 14:14–16) and one that is damning (14:17–20), are more persuasive.[23] It is clear that the grape harvest (14:17–20) denotes judgment since we are told that God's wrath is revealed in the treading of the winepress (14:19). In addition, the blood flowing up to horses' bridles leaves no doubt that we have a description of judgment (14:20). The references to the winepress also allude to Old Testament texts that clearly denote God's judgment (Isa. 63:2; Jer. 48:33; Joel 3:13). Nevertheless, the harvest in Revelation 14:14–16 should not be equated with the grape harvest but should be understood to refer to salvation for the following reasons.

First, this harvest is conducted by the Son of Man rather than an angel, which suggests that it has a different purpose and result, namely, salvation instead of judgment. Second, there is no clear reference to God's wrath or judgment in 14:14–16, which again suggests that God's judgment isn't intended. The clear references to judgment found in the grape harvest (14:17–20) are lacking in the first harvest (14:14–16). Third, the image of the harvest doesn't invariably signify judgment, for the harvest may also designate the gathering in of those who are saved (Matt. 9:37–38; John 4:35–38), and we see in Matthew 13:30 that at the final harvest the wicked are burned and the righteous delivered. Galatians 6:7–8 moves in the same orbit; the final judgment is compared to the harvest, and some "will from the flesh reap

21 Tabb, *All Things New*, 52.
22 See Eckhard J. Schnabel, "John and the Future of the Nations," *BBR* 12, no. 2 (2002): 257–62.
23 Cf. Bauckham, *Theology of Revelation*, 94–98; Bauckham, *Climax of Prophecy*, 283–96; Koester, *Revelation*, 623–24, 628–29. I am not persuaded by the claim that the death of the martyrs anticipates a harvest of the nations in the future.

corruption," but others "will from the Spirit reap eternal life." Thus, the metaphor of the harvest fits with the notion of salvation. Fourth, it seems more probable that the two harvests don't convey the same truth, since otherwise, the two texts seem unnecessarily repetitive. We see in this text, then, that the Son of Man doesn't come first to judge but to harvest and save a people.

We also see that Jesus is an exemplar of salvation, as a "faithful witness" (Rev. 1:5), and this theme is picked up elsewhere (3:14). Antipas also functions as a "faithful witness" (2:13), but Jesus is surely the exemplar par excellence, in that he remained faithful to God until death (cf. 2:10), even his death by crucifixion. The church is called to suffer, but the suffering it experiences is never greater than the suffering endured by her Lord and Christ. Even though Jesus is not called the brother of fellow believers, we see his solidarity with his people in the suffering he faced, and thus the call for the church to persevere in suffering is not a distant exhortation from one who never suffered himself.

Jesus's atoning death secures forgiveness for those who belong to him. Indeed, the centrality of the cross in Revelation stands out, showing that the fundamental message of Revelation harmonizes with the rest of the New Testament, which focuses on Jesus as the crucified and risen Lord who died and rose for the forgiveness of sins. In the "grace and peace" wish, Jesus is introduced as the one "who loves us and has freed from our sins by his blood" (1:5). A variant reading says that he has "washed" (Gk. *lousanti*) us of our sins rather than "freed" (Gk. *lusanti*) us from them. The difference is only one letter in Greek. Although the image of washing away sins is vivid and attractive, the best manuscript evidence supports the reading "freed" instead of "washed." We see, then, that the centrality of the cross is featured from the outset of the book. The beleaguered church is strengthened and fortified to suffer, hearing of Jesus's love for them and that his love moved him to give his life for their sake. We find a similar sentiment in 1 John 4:10: "In this is love, not that we have loved God, but that he loved us and sent his Son to be the propitiation for our sins." The term translated "freed" in Revelation 1:5 could also be rendered "released," and what we find here is exodus language, deliverance imagery, which emphasizes liberation from the sin that enslaves and dominates unbelievers.

The most significant text for Jesus's atoning work in Revelation is found in chapter 5. Chapter 4 contains the awesome and terrifying vision of God seated on his throne with thousands upon thousands worshiping him. Chapter 5 commences with God on his throne holding a scroll with seven seals. An angel with a thunderous voice asks, "Who is worthy to open the scroll and break its seals?" (5:2). The word "worthy" (Gk. *axios*) plays a crucial role in the chapter and in the entire book. The answer given is that no one in the created universe, whether human or angelic, is able to open the seven-sealed book. John weeps because "no one is found worthy to open the scroll or even to look into it" (5:4). We see from the entire narrative in the book of Revelation that if the scroll isn't opened, then the redemption of the human race will not be accomplished, and God's purposes for his creation will not be realized.

John slows down the narrative, relaying step-by-step what happens so that readers sense how momentous it is that no one in the universe is worthy to open the scroll. One of the elders interrupts John's weeping and tells him that one is able to open the scroll (5:5). The Lion from Judah's tribe, "the Root of David," is qualified to open the scroll and break its seals. I commented earlier on the significance of Jesus being the promised Messiah, the Son of David. Here we see that he is able to break the seals because of his royalty and majesty and strength as the Lion, as the mighty King of Israel.

The narrative, however, takes a surprising and beautiful turn. As many commentators have noted, John is *told* about a Lion, but when he *looks*, he sees a Lamb, a Lamb that has been slain (5:6).[24] The significance of the vision can hardly be overstated, for John is telling us as readers that Jesus is both a Lion and a Lamb, but he conquered and triumphed not as a Lion but as a Lamb. The victory over evil was won not through overwhelming force but through loving self-sacrifice and surrender.[25]

24 See here Bauckham, *Climax of Prophecy*, 180.
25 Caird, *Revelation*, 75; Osborne, *Revelation*, 254; Bauckham, *Climax of Prophecy*, 183.

It isn't as if all violence and force are renounced, because there will be a final judgment, which the book of Revelation emphasizes frequently. But before that judgment, there is salvation and an offer of repentance. The judgment falls on those who refuse love, on those who continue to pursue evil and who worship the beast instead of the one true God.

Even though the word for "Lamb" used here (Gk. *arnion*) differs from what we see in John's Gospel (Gk. *amnos*), the Revelation 5 passage reminds us of John 1:29: "Behold, the Lamb of God, who takes away the sin of the world." The lamb imagery in Revelation could come from the sacrifices offered to procure atonement in the temple cult, or perhaps the background is the Passover lamb (Ex. 12:1–49).[26] Some see a reference to the innocent lamb of Isaiah 53:7. Decisive evidence to distinguish between these options is lacking, and perhaps we should see all three as the background—in this case John draws on Old Testament tradition more generally.[27] Such a state of affairs would not be surprising, because the reference to the lamb in Isaiah 53 reflects sacrificial tradition, particularly the idea that the servant gave his life as "an offering for guilt" (Isa. 53:10).

John emphasizes that Jesus is "worthy" as the slain Lamb and that by his death he accomplished redemption for his people. Indeed, he is worthy to break the seals and open the scroll, "for" (Gk. *hoti*) he was slain (Rev. 5:9), and by his death, by means of his blood, he purchased some from every people group on earth. The word translated by the ESV as "ransomed" (Gk. *agorazō*) could also be rendered "redeemed," and thus Jesus's blood functions as the price of redemption. The word "blood" has sacrificial associations, for in the Old Testament cult, the shedding of the blood of animals secured forgiveness of sins. The relationship between blood and forgiveness is evident in Leviticus 17:11: "For the life of the flesh is in the blood, and I have given it for

---

26 So Bauckham, *Theology of Revelation*, 70–71; Beale, *Revelation*, 351. Beale also includes the suffering servant of Isa. 53. For a careful investigation of the background, see David E. Aune, *Revelation 1–5*, WBC 52A (Nashville: Thomas Nelson, 1997), 367–73.

27 For the general nature of the background for the term "Lamb," see Koester, *Revelation*, 386.

you on the altar to make atonement for your souls, for it is the blood
that makes atonement by the life."[28] The verb for "atonement" is *kipper*
in the Hebrew and *hilaskomai* in Greek. The verb has to do with the
appeasement or the satisfaction of God's wrath.[29] Gordon Wenham sees
the "principle of substitution" here, for "animal life takes the place of
human life."[30] We should not conceive of blood as having a mystical
quality that atones. The shedding of one's blood, as anyone who lived
in the ancient world keenly recognized, signifies that one has died. The
sacrifice of blood indicates that one's life has been violently taken away.[31]

We see here why the atoning death of Jesus is so important. I have
argued elsewhere that Adam and Eve were created to rule the world
under God's lordship, but they squandered and lost that rule through
their rebellious defiance.[32] Jesus has ransomed his own, however, and
has made them "a kingdom and priests to our God, / and they shall
reign on the earth" (Rev. 5:10). The sacrificial death of the Lamb has
obtained the rule intended for human beings. Forgiveness of sins is

28 Rightly, Angel Manuel Rodriguez, "Substitution in the Hebrew Cultus and in Cultic-
Related Texts," (PhD diss., Andrews University Seventh-Day Adventist Theological
Seminary, 1979), 233–57; J. Alan Groves, "Atonement in Isaiah 53: 'For He Bore the Sins
of Many,'" in *The Glory of the Atonement: Biblical, Historical, and Practical Perspectives;
Essays in Honor of Roger Nicole*, ed. Charles E. Hill and Frank A. James III (Downers Grove,
IL: IVP Academic, 2004), 65–68. Contra Jacob Milgrom, *Leviticus 1–16: A New Transla-
tion with Introduction and Commentary*, AB 3 (New York: Doubleday, 1991), 1082–83;
Milgrom attempts to segregate cultic from noncultic texts. The substitutionary character
of the Hebrew verb *kipper* is defended by Emile Nicole, "Atonement in the Pentateuch:
'It is the Blood That Makes Atonement for One's Life,'" in Hill and James, *Glory of the
Atonement*, 47–50. See also David Peterson, "Atonement in the Old Testament," in *Where
Wrath and Mercy Meet: Proclaiming the Atonement Today*, ed. David Peterson (Carlisle,
UK: Paternoster, 2001), 10–12.
29 The sacrifice of Noah after the flood communicates the idea that the sacrifice averted God's
wrath (Gen. 8:21). So Gordon J. Wenham, "The Theology of Old Testament Sacrifice,"
in *Sacrifice in the Bible*, ed. Roger T. Beckwith and Martin J. Selman (Grand Rapids, MI:
Baker, 1995), 80–81.
30 Wenham, "Old Testament Sacrifice," 82; cf. Nicole, "Atonement in the Pentateuch," 35–50,
esp. 36–40.
31 See especially Leon Morris, *The Apostolic Preaching of the Cross*, 3rd ed. (Grand Rapids,
MI: Eerdmans, 1965), 112–28; Nicole, "Atonement in the Pentateuch," 39–40, 46.
32 Thomas R. Schreiner, *The King in His Beauty: A Biblical Theology of the Old and New
Testaments* (Grand Rapids, MI: Baker Academic, 2013), 5–11.

fundamental and foundational, but God's other intentions in securing forgiveness should not be neglected. Forgiveness restores human beings to the calling that was first given to Adam and Eve. In the death of Jesus we have both substitution and Christus Victor. Christus Victor emphasizes that Jesus has triumphed over sin, death, and the devil. He has freed us from slavery so that we can live as God intends. Just as Adam and Eve were kings and priests in the garden, now believers rule in an inaugurated fashion and as priests mediate God's blessing to the world.

John doesn't explicitly say that Jesus's death was substitutionary, but such a notion, as suggested above, is surely present. We see elsewhere in Revelation that judgment will be the destiny of those who fail to repent, of those who because of their hard hearts don't turn from their sin. Those who are redeemed and purchased are liberated because Jesus shed his blood, which indicates that he gave his life for theirs. Such a notion is the most natural way of understanding the sacrifices in the Old Testament cult. The laying of one's hand on an animal symbolizes the transfer of sin from the person to the animal (e.g., Lev. 16:21–22). Wenham remarks, "What he [the worshiper] does to the animal, he does symbolically to himself. The death of the animal portrays the death of himself."[33] Some object that the referent in Leviticus 16:21–22 was a live goat, and this is a helpful observation. Nevertheless, the goat was probably sent into the wilderness to die.[34] Geerhardus Vos insightfully says that both goats on the Day of Atonement must be taken together to understand the truth about atonement, for there was

in reality one sacrificial object; the distribution of suffering death and of dismissal into a remote place simply serving the purpose of clearer expression, in visible form, of removal of sin after expiation

---

33 Wenham, "Old Testament Sacrifice," 77. He proceeds to say, "The animal is a substitute of the worshipper. Its death makes atonement for the worshipper. Its immolation on the altar quietens God's anger at human sin." Wenham, 82.

34 See Peterson, "Atonement in the Old Testament," 15; Garry Williams, "The Cross and the Punishment of Sin," in Peterson, *Where Wrath and Mercy Meet*, 79.

had been made, something which the ordinary sacrificial animal could not well express, since it died in the process of expiation.[35]

John does not specifically tell us why Jesus's death makes him "worthy" to break the seals, to redeem human beings, and to restore them to their role as kings and priests, but the answer is implicit in the storyline of Revelation 5. He is worthy because he is the Messiah, the Davidic King, and as the King, he represents his people. At the end of the chapter, the angelic multitudes sing praise to the slain Lamb, saying that he deserves "honor and glory and blessing" (5:12). Indeed, we saw above that in 5:13 he is specifically praised just as God is praised and honored, and he is worshiped (5:14) just as God is worshiped (4:10).[36] We find here, then, another reason why the Lamb can atone for sins, for he is both human, as the Davidic King, and divine, as one who shares in God's identity. He is the God-man, and thus his death for sinners is efficacious. When Athanasius wrote the classic *On the Incarnation*, contending that Jesus Christ had to be fully divine and fully human to atone for sins, he was not deviating from the New Testament witness but was remaining faithful to what the New Testament itself teaches.

Another feature of the narrative, which has been neglected thus far, is that the Lamb that was slain is standing (5:6). Standing represents the resurrection, indicating that death didn't triumph over Jesus Christ and that forgiveness and victory are achieved through both the death and resurrection.[37] Jesus purchased people for God as the crucified and risen Lord. Along the same lines, Jesus is designated "the firstborn of the dead" and "the ruler of kings on earth" (1:5), and in 1:5–6, we have a doxology to Jesus, even as doxologies are restricted to God.[38] The phrase "firstborn of/from the dead" appears in Colossians as well (Col. 1:18), signifying in both Revelation and Colossians Jesus's sovereignty over

---

35 Geerhardus Vos, *Biblical Theology: Old and New Testaments* (Grand Rapids, MI: Eerdmans, 1977), 163. I owe this citation to Nicole, "Atonement in the Pentateuch," 26–27.

36 Cf. Hofius, *Neutestamentliche Studien*, 232; Beale, *Revelation*, 365–66.

37 The slain Lamb is also the conquering Lamb. So Osborne, *Revelation*, 682–88; Beale, *Revelation*, 958–60; Koester, *Revelation*, 386.

38 Hofius, *Neutestamentliche Studien*, 22.

death, since he is the first one resurrected. The resurrection in Jewish thought is indissolubly connected with the arrival of the new age, the coming of the new creation. When we read about the resurrection in Isaiah 25:6–8; 26:19; Ezekiel 37; and Daniel 12:2–3, it signals the restoration of Israel, the triumph of goodness, and the defeat of evil. The age of life and paradise begins with the resurrection. We see again that Jesus's cross and resurrection together constitute redemption, and interestingly, the cross and resurrection in Revelation 1:6, as in 5:10, have "made us a kingdom, priests to his God and Father." The work of redemption doesn't end with forgiveness but frees believers to carry out the purpose for which they were first created.[39]

Jesus's rule over death is also featured in the vision of the Son of Man. In Daniel 7, the "son of man" approaches the Ancient of Days to receive a kingdom, and three times Daniel informs us that the saints receive the kingdom and the rule (Dan. 7:18, 22, 27), which indicates that the "son of man" is the corporate head of the saints.[40] John reminds us that there is no place for fear, since Jesus assures him, "I am . . . the living one. I died, and behold I am alive forevermore, and I have the keys of Death and Hades" (Rev. 1:17–18). As Otfried Hofius points out, in the Old Testament Yahweh is often designated "the living God,"[41] and Jesus's death spells the defeat of death forever, so that the kingdom promise is realized fully with the utter destruction of "Death" and "Hades" as apocalyptic powers that oppress human beings (20:14). The annihilation of Death and Hades is fittingly portrayed in 20:14, where we are told that "Death and Hades were thrown into the lake of fire." Death and Hades cannot claim final victory since they are part of the old creation that will be quashed and removed from the realm of the new creation on the basis of Jesus's death and resurrection.

---

39 Believers are already reigning, though the consummation of their reign is a future reality. Tabb, *All Things New*, 91–92.

40 For a defense of this view, see Thomas R. Schreiner, *New Testament Theology: Magnifying God in Christ* (Grand Rapids, MI: Baker Academic, 2008), 214–16.

41 Hofius, *Neutestamentliche Studien*, 227–28.

The cosmic nature of the Lamb's victory emerges in chapter 7 as well. There John answers a question posed at the end of chapter 6, as the wrath of the one sitting on the throne and the wrath of the Lamb are highlighted. Because the day of their wrath is approaching, the question that arises is "Who can stand?" (6:17). The angels are then instructed to delay injuring the earth and sea until God's servants are sealed (7:1–3). The harm inflicted by the angels is another way of describing the final judgment that is coming. God's servants are described as the 144,000 from every tribe of Israel, and John proceeds to enumerate 12,000 sealed from twelve different tribes.

Excursus on the 144,000

We delve into the meaning of the 144,000 here, and readers uninterested in technical details can skip ahead to the next section. Some interpreters, from the dispensationalist tradition, and other traditions as well, claim that the 144,000 are Jewish believers, but I will argue that this is an unlikely reading. Instead, the 144,000 should be identified, both here and in Revelation 14:1–5, as all those redeemed by Jesus Christ.[a] In other words, the 144,000 designate both Jewish and Gentile believers. The following arguments support the interpretation defended here.

First, the wrath threatened in 6:15–17 is the wrath poured out on the day of the Lord, which represents the final judgment, as defended previously in this book. John asks who can be spared from that wrath, and it hardly makes sense for those spared to be limited to the Jewish people.[b] John considers *all* those who are delivered from the impending wrath, for just as the wrath is worldwide, so too is the deliverance.

Second, those sealed are God's "servants" (Gk. *doulous*, 7:3), but as in 1:1; 19:2, 5; 22:3; and 22:6, his servants represent all those who belong to God, all those who will receive the final reward.

Third, in an apocalyptic book, we are not surprised that Israel and its tribes have a spiritual meaning. Twice we are told that the Jews are a "synagogue of Satan" (2:9; 3:9), while the true people of God consists of believers in Jesus Christ. Such a description of Jewish opponents, of course, must not be used to justify anti-Semitism, nor would John countenance such abuse of his words.[c] John addresses a situation in which Jews were persecuting Christians; they were probably reporting believers to imperial authorities, which led to persecution. John turns the tables on those in the Jewish synagogue, saying that believers in Jesus, in contrast to unbelieving Jews, are the true people of God. The key text is Revelation 3:9, where we find allusions to several Old Testament texts. In Psalm 86:9, the psalmist predicts that the pagan nations of the world will come and bow before Yahweh and give worship and glory to him. Similarly, in Isaiah 60:14, pagans who oppressed and mistreated Israel will confess that Jerusalem is the Lord's city. And in Isaiah 49:23, pagan kings and queens will nurture Israel, bow before the Jews, and lick the dust of their feet. John appropriates these Old Testament texts in a stunning way, concluding from them that ethnic Jews will bow at the feet of believers in Jesus Christ and acknowledge that Gentile and Jewish believers are beloved. In other words, the true Jews, the restored Israel, consists of those who put their faith and trust in Jesus. Such a reading fits with the conception that the 144,000 in Israel represent the church of Jesus Christ.[d]

Fourth, it seems to some that the 144,000 with the enumerated listing of 12,000 from twelve different tribes must refer to ethnic Israel. But the number twelve should give us pause because it has symbolic significance since Israel consisted of twelve tribes and Jesus appointed twelve apostles—most agree that the twelve apostles constitute the nucleus of the new people of God. When we add to this the apocalyptic character of the book of Revelation and its characteristic use of numbers, we have good reasons to think the number is symbolic. Our suspicion that the number is symbolic increases when we recognize that the number 144,000 is 12 x 12 x 1,000. It seems quite unlikely that such numbers should be read literally.

This brings us to the fifth point, for someone might say that the number is symbolic but that the referent is still ethnic Israel since we have the enumeration of 12,000 from twelve distinct tribes in Israel. But when we look at the tribes listed and compare it with the listing of the tribes in the Old Testament, we have no other example in which the twelve tribes are listed as they are here. John hints that we should not understand the tribes literally because both Manasseh and Joseph are listed, and they represent the same tribe. In addition, the tribe of Dan is absent, and thus it is difficult to see how the listing can represent ethnic Israel when one tribe is entirely missing. Significantly, Judah is listed first, probably because Jesus as the Messiah is from the tribe of Judah (cf. Rev. 5:5). The listing of the twelve tribes suggests that the church of Jesus Christ is the true Israel, the fulfilled Israel. John sees the church not as the replacement of Israel but as the fulfillment of God's promises to Israel in which Israel is redefined. The listing of the tribes echoes the book of Numbers, where the tribes are counted for war (Num. 1–2), suggesting that the church of Jesus Christ represents the Lord's army in the world, although it is an army pursuing peace.[e]

Sixth, another indication that the 144,000 are not literally Israelites is the juxtaposition of Revelation 7:4–8 and 7:9–17. We saw a similar circumstance in chapter 5, where John was *told* about the Lion from the tribe of Judah, but when he *looked*, he saw a Lamb (5:5–6). In chapter 7, John *hears* about the 144,000 sealed from the twelve tribes of Israel (7:4), but when he *looks*, he sees an uncountable number from every tribe, language, and nation (7:9).[f] We saw in chapter 5 that the Lion and the Lamb have the *same referent*: Jesus Christ. So too here the 144,000 and the uncountable multitude refer to the same entity: the worldwide church of Jesus Christ. The literary device used confirms that the number 144,000 is symbolic, referring to the entire people of God—to the uncountable multitudes who believe. In the same way, the uncountable multitude is the true and fulfilled Israel, the people of God.

Seventh, several arguments from 14:1–5, where the 144,000 are standing with the Lamb on Mount Zion, strengthen the notion that we have a symbolic description of the church of Jesus Christ. First, the 144,000 have the name of the Lamb and the Father inscribed on their foreheads (14:1), and most would agree that the writing here is symbolic instead of literal. But the main point here is not the symbolic nature of the engraving. Instead, the name imprinted on the foreheads signifies that the 144,000 belong to the Lamb and to the Father. They stand in contrast to the earth dwellers, who have the mark of the beast on their foreheads and hands (13:16–17). Indeed, in 14:9–11, we are told in the strongest terms that those who receive the beast's mark will suffer torment and punishment forever. This brings us to what is germane to the discussion on the identity of the 144,000. It is quite unlikely that those who have the name of the Lamb and the Father on their foreheads are restricted to Israel. It is much more natural to see a reference to all believers, both Jews and Gentiles, who have refused to compromise with the beast. John comforts not only Jewish believers in Asia Minor but all believers in the seven cities addressed.

In addition, the remainder of the paragraph (14:2–5) confirms this reading. The 144,000 sing "a new song" (14:3), and in 5:9, the new song is linked with the Lamb purchasing some from every tribe, language, and people. In the Old Testament, a new song is hymned when God's people experience his saving work on their behalf (Pss. 40:3; 96:1; 98:1; 144:9; Isa. 42:10). In Revelation we are informed that the new song is restricted to the 144,000 who are "redeemed from the earth" (Rev. 14:3). Those "redeemed from the earth" is a universal statement and most naturally refers to *all* those who are redeemed. Some might object that in the next verse the 144,000 are designated the "firstfruits" (14:4), which suggests that others are redeemed apart from them. On this scenario the firstfruits refer to Gentile believers who confess faith after the Jews. But we have no indication elsewhere in Revelation of a temporal relationship between Jewish and Gentile believers so that Jews are saved first and then Gentiles. Instead, the redemption of all believers is the firstfruits, but the rest of humanity, which is not part of the firstfruits, is not dedicated to God and is thus judged as unbelieving.[g]

We should note as well that the symbolic language that dominates the paragraph also points to a figurative reading of the 144,000. For instance, the 144,000 are said to be virgins who did not defile themselves with women (14:4), and some have taken this description literally. But that conception actually contradicts what we read elsewhere in the New Testament. Paul attributes the notion that marriage defiles to a demonic source (1 Tim. 4:1–3), which suggests that in an apocalyptic book like Revelation we should read a reference to virginity figuratively. John draws on the Old Testament ideas that Israel belongs to Yahweh alone as his bride and that consorting with any other god is spiritual harlotry (Isa. 57:3–5; Jer. 2:20; 3:1–10; 13:27;

Ezek. 16:1–63; 20:30–32; 23:1–49; Hos. 1:1–3:5; 4:10–18; 5:3–4; 6:10; 9:1).[h] We find the same notion when Paul says to the Corinthians, "I betrothed you to one husband, to present you as a pure virgin to Christ" (2 Cor. 11:2). Back in Revelation 14, John goes on to explain what he means by this reference to virgins: the redeemed "follow the Lamb wherever he goes" (14:4), and here we have an echo of the Gospel of John, where Jesus's flock follows him as the good shepherd (John 10:4, 5, 27). Similarly, the blamelessness and lack of lying are symbolic. Lying, in the Old Testament, is described as idolatry (cf. Ps. 4:3; Isa. 28:15, 17; Jer. 3:23; Hos. 11:12). Isaiah ridicules the idolatry of his day, saying about the idolater, "He feeds on ashes; a deluded heart has led him astray, and he cannot deliver himself or say, 'Is there not a lie in my right hand?'" (Isa. 44:20). In the same way, the 144,000 are blameless (cf. Eph. 5:27; Col. 1:22; Jude 24), which should not be equated with sinlessness; they are blameless because they refuse to participate in idolatry.

The eighth and last argument comes from outside the text. After the Assyrian exile in 722 BC, most in the northern tribes, it seems, lost their identity (but see Luke 2:36). The tribal structure of Israel is connected to occupying the land, but the northern tribes forfeited their tie to the land when they were exiled to Assyria. Thus it became increasingly difficult to identify one's tribe since the tribal nature of Israel was lost; Israel scattered and intermarried, and it seems doubtful that careful records were kept, especially among those who had fallen away from the Lord and who intermarried with ethnic groups outside Israel. The problem is especially difficult if the text is seen as a prophecy about the future salvation of ethnic Israel. Very few Israelites today know the tribe from which they originated, and it seems that those who argue for a literal reading of the passage have to say that the 12,000 chosen from each tribe are known to God, even if they themselves don't know which tribe they come from. Such a scenario seems strange because God would have to reveal supernaturally to Israelites their tribe if the 12,000 from each tribe were to be known on earth.

a   So also Beale, *Revelation*, 412–13, 16–23; Bauckham, *Theology of Revelation*, 77; Bauckham, *Climax of Prophecy*, 180; Koester, *Revelation*, 427.
b   Cf. Caird, *Revelation*, 95.
c   Aune notes that similar expressions are used in disputes among Jews at Qumran and in Jewish testamentary literature. *Revelation 1–5*, 164–65.
d   Against Beale, there is no reference to the end-time salvation of Jews here. *Revelation*, 287–88.
e   Cf. Caird, *Revelation*, 96; Bauckham, *Theology of Revelation*, 77.
f   Cf. Bauckham, *Theology of Revelation*, 76–77.
g   See Beale, *Revelation*, 744; Koester, *Revelation*, 619.
h   Perhaps we also have a reference here to the heavenly army and to the requirement to remain sexually abstinent when going to war (Deut. 23:9–14; 1 Sam. 21:5; 2 Sam. 11:9–13; 1QM 7.3–6). So Bauckham, *Theology of Revelation*, 78.

Sealing and Washing of the 144,000

The 144,000 are said to be sealed (Rev. 7:4), and the sealing means that the 144,000—the church of Jesus Christ—are protected from the day of wrath that is coming. Those who are sealed are those who are able to stand when God's wrath flashes forth (6:17). Or as chapter 14 says, they are those who are "redeemed" (14:3–4), and the language of redemption (Gk. *agorazō*) points back to 5:9, where the Lamb has purchased some from every people group in the world. The 144,000 are sealed, protected from God's wrath, because they are purchased by the Lamb's blood.

The narrative in chapter 7 supports the same conclusion. We have already seen that the 144,000 sealed and the uncountable multitude refer to the same entity. They are those clothed in white robes (7:13), and white robes designate those who belong to God, those who are righteous and who can stand in God's presence (3:4, 5, 18; 6:11; 7:9;

19:14). In chapter 7, one of the elders queries John, asking him about those in white robes and where they come from (7:13). The elder explains to John that those clothed with white robes have come "out of the great tribulation" (7:14). The "great tribulation" refers not to the last seven years of history nor to three and one-half years at the end of history but to the entire period between the resurrection and the second coming.[42] Those in white robes have emerged from life on earth, from "many dangers, toils, and snares,"[43] and now they are in God's presence forever in the new creation (7:15–17) since their robes are white. John tells us how their robes were whitened: "They have washed their robes and made them white in the blood of the Lamb" (7:14).

Richard Bauckham reads this verse to say that their robes are whitened through martyrdom, through their devotion to Christ.[44] Such a conception makes sense in that the white robes refer to the godliness of believers elsewhere in the book. Still, the context points in another direction since here the robes of believers are whitened through *washing*, and they are washed by the Lamb's blood, which signifies that the uncountable multitude is clothed with white garments because of the cleansing achieved by Christ's sacrifice.[45] The clothing of the uncountable multitude is whitened by means of the Lamb's blood (Gk. *en tō haimati tou arniou*), showing that in this context the clothes aren't made white by the righteous lives of believers. When we consider the contribution of Revelation as a whole, those who have their clothing whitened through the Lamb's blood also live righteous lives. But the cleansing accomplished by the Lamb is the basis and foundation for a new life. We should read 22:14—where John says, "Blessed are those who wash their robes, so that they may have the right to the tree of life and that they may enter the city by the gates"—in light of 7:14. Both verses have the same word for "washing" (Gk. *plynō*) and the same

---

42 Koester, *Revelation*, 429.

43 John Newton, "Amazing Grace," 1779.

44 Bauckham, *Climax of Prophecy*, 228–29; Bauckham, *Theology of Revelation*, 77.

45 See Beale, *Revelation*, 436–48; Osborne, *Revelation*, 325–26. Cf. Koester, *Revelation*, 430. Perhaps this is an allusion to washing robes in blood from Gen. 49:11; see Tabb, *All Things New*, 57.

word for "robes" (Gk. *stolas*). In 7:14, those with washed robes have access to the new temple (7:15–17), which is the new creation and the new Jerusalem (21:1–22:5), while in 22:14 those with washed robes have access to the tree of life and the heavenly city. In other words, in both cases washed robes bring an everlasting reward. And the many points of contact between the two texts demonstrate that the washed robes refer to the cleansing accomplished through Christ's blood. In a picturesque and beautiful fashion, we see that Christ's death unlocks the key that allows entrance to the city of life.

The Dragon Cast Out

One of the most important and dramatic chapters in Revelation is chapter 12, where John pulls back the curtain and shows us the cosmic conflict that explains and unpacks what is happening on earth. The scene is set with strange and wondrous signs in heaven. We see a woman shining with the sun, having a crown of twelve stars with the moon under her feet (12:1). We might think the woman enjoyed a blissful reign far above the stresses and strains of life on earth, but she suffers the anguish of birth pangs (12:2). Suddenly another sign appears in heaven, "a great red dragon" who also has all the lineaments of rule (12:3). Some think the hurling of stars to the earth refers to the fall of angels who rebelled along with Satan (12:4), but the verse alludes to Daniel 8:10, where Antiochus IV Epiphanes threw stars to the ground, with the stars representing those in Israel persecuted by Antiochus. So too here the stars represent believers persecuted by the dragon. But the dragon's greatest desire is to destroy and murder the child of the woman (Rev. 12:4), the Christ, for in doing so, he would vanquish any hope of salvation. We think, for instance, of Herod's attempt to slay the Christ child in the Matthean account (Matt. 2:1–12). John tells the story of salvation here in sweeping terms and doesn't pause to relay details as he chronicles the cosmic drama. The son of the woman is born, and John alludes to Psalm 2, which relates the rage and rebellion of the nations against the anointed Messiah of Israel (Ps. 2:1–3). We also have an allusion to Psalm 2:9, where the Christ rules over the nations with an iron rod, and he rules, as Revelation 12:5 shows, because he is the exalted and ascended one. John zooms from Jesus's birth to his final victory, showing us in a sneak preview the end of the story, the culmination of the cosmic conflict. Jesus the Christ reigns as the risen one, as the exalted one, and thus he enjoys dominion and authority over the dragon. Jesus rules and reigns as the Christ in heaven, but the woman, who represents the people of God, flees to the wilderness, where she is nourished and protected by God (12:6). She resides in the wilderness for 1,260 days, a time that starts with Jesus's resurrection and ends when Jesus returns.

John does not explain in the first panel of his sketch, in 12:1–6, how the Son triumphed over the dragon, but in the second panel (12:7–12), he clarifies how victory was accomplished. A window is opened into the heavenly realms, where we see a war break out between Michael and his angels, on the one hand, and the dragon and his angels, on the other. John neglects the details of the battle entirely, and such a strange and mysterious conflict in heaven piques our curiosity as readers. Nevertheless, John zeroes in on the outcome of the battle, in which the dragon and his angels are thrown out of heaven (12:7–9). Satan's being cast out of heaven doesn't refer to an event before the fall of Adam and Eve, nor does it hark back to a time in primeval history when angels defected and joined up with Satan. John isn't attempting to give us a window into primeval history; he shows no interest in Revelation about the origin of Satan or about how he originally fell into sin, nor is there any evidence in the context that he casts his eye backward to the beginning of time. Instead, the defeat of Satan, as the next panel reveals (12:10–12), is accomplished at the cross. The interpretation defended here also fits with the first six verses (12:1–6), in which Jesus escapes the dragon's clutches and triumphs over him through his exaltation as the risen and reigning King.

We saw in an earlier chapter that believers must "conquer" (Gk. *nikaō*) to obtain an eternal reward (2:7, 11, 17, 26; 3:5, 12, 21; 15:2; 21:7), but here the ultimate reason they conquer and overcome is traced to "the blood of the Lamb" (12:11). We should not extend the

Lamb's blood here to include the martyrdom of believers, for that is the subject of the next lines. In this way, the fundamental and foundational character of Christ's death is preserved.[46] Believers *conquer* because "the Lion from the tribe of Judah . . . has *conquered*" (5:5). Our victory is rooted in his victory; Christ's death on the cross is the basis for the triumph of the saints. We have an apocalyptic version here of what we read in John 12:31, where Jesus anticipates that at his death, "the ruler of this world"—Satan—"[will] be cast out" (Gk. *eklblēthēsetai*). In Revelation 12, the verb is "throw out" (Gk. *ballō*), but the concept is the same. The serpent, the devil, Satan, the mighty dragon has been ejected from heaven, but his defeat comes not through overwhelming force, nor even by the strength of Michael, but through the suffering and death of the Son of God. Jesus reigns and rules (12:5) as the suffering Messiah, as the one who is the victor over all evil powers through his death. The atoning death of Jesus has also removed the basis for Satan's accusations against believers (12:11), which suggests that Jesus's death effects forgiveness of sins. Believers are stabbed in their consciences as they consider their sins, but the accusations of the devil have no standing any longer because the sins of believers are expunged by virtue of Jesus's cleansing death.

Jesus's Return

Jesus reigns as the exalted one, as the ruler of all (Rev. 12:5), since he is the Son of Man who received the kingdom from the Father (1:12–16). Jesus's reign from heaven should not be confused with the consummation. At the inception and conclusion of the book of Revelation we are told that "the time is near" (1:3; 22:10), and the time in view is the end of the present world order.[47] Along the same lines, we are informed that Jesus is coming soon (3:11; 22:7, 12, 20). Some interpret this to say that

---

46 Against Caird, *Revelation*, 156; Bauckham, *Theology of Revelation*, 75–76. Rightly, Koester, *Revelation*, 565.

47 Caird emphasizes the nearness of persecution, but a reference to Christ's second coming and the consummation of history is more convincing. *Revelation*, 12. See Aune, *Revelation 1–5*, 21; Osborne, *Revelation*, 59.

he will come quickly when he comes, but such an interpretation can be dismissed as highly unlikely. It seems faintly ridiculous to imagine John to be saying that when Jesus returns, his descent will be rapid instead of slow. Others think that all the coming texts refer to the destruction of Jerusalem in AD 70, but Jerusalem plays an insignificant role in the book as a whole, and John betrays little interest in the fate of the city historically. All the sayings about Jesus coming soon are tied to the eschatological consummation, though some interpreters think that 2:5, 16; 3:3, 11; and 16:15 refer to comings in history.[48] Such a reading of 16:15 is doubtful since the threat of his coming (and it is a threat in this context) occurs in the same context in which Armageddon (16:16) is predicted. Similarly, in 3:11, Jesus's coming is linked with believers receiving a crown and the promise of dwelling in the new temple.[49]

Other interpreters claim that we have the promise of returning soon but that the events of history have falsified John's claim. In other words, John got it wrong. We can certainly understand such a conclusion, for readers two thousand years down the road are naturally puzzled and perplexed about what it means for Jesus to come soon. There are no easy answers, but those who read the Scriptures canonically (and surely if any book should be read canonically, it is Revelation, since it is rightly placed as the last book in the canon) recognize that there are similar claims in other books.

We see an illuminating parallel in Isaiah 40–66. The most natural reading of Isaiah 40–66 is that the return of Israel from the exile in Babylon will fulfill all the promises Yahweh made to Israel. The new creation will dawn (Isa. 65:17–22; 66:22), Israel will shine with glorious light and all nations will come to her (Isa. 60:1–22), and Jerusalem will be exalted (Isa. 62:1–12). The stunning promises given to Israel in Isaiah 40–66, however, were scarcely fulfilled in their fullness in the return from exile (though Israel did return from exile), and yet readers hundreds of years later do not reject the Isaianic witness; indeed, they

48 See Caird, *Revelation*, 32; Mounce, *Revelation*, 89; Beale, *Revelation*, 232–33.
49 See Osborne, *Revelation*, 118. Koester thinks the text suggests both comings, so that we cannot limit what is said here to a present or final coming. *Revelation*, 331–32.

see the words of Isaiah fulfilled, or at least beginning to be fulfilled, in the ministry, death, and resurrection of Jesus the Messiah. The truth of Isaiah's prophecy was not denied by Jesus and the apostles, even though the time of fulfillment does not match the presumable understanding of Isaiah's first readers.

I am not claiming that such an example entirely solves the promise that Jesus will come soon in Revelation. The point is that in the canon of Scripture, previous prophecies and the delay in their fulfillment should shape our understanding of what it means for Jesus to come soon. We need to recognize as well that the matter is quite complex, so that simplistic answers should be eschewed. Some indications of an interval of time exist in the book,[50] and thus the martyrs are told to wait because more must be slain before the end (Rev. 6:9–11). Also, saying the woman will be preserved in the wilderness for 1,260 days (12:6) or for "a time, and times, and half a time" (12:14) points to some delay before the end of history, as does the trampling of the holy city for forty-two months (11:2) and the ministry of the two witnesses for 1,260 days (11:3). Another piece of evidence is that the fifth king reigns (17:10), and the end won't come before the seventh king arrives (17:10–11).

We see a similar eschatological tension in the Gospel of Luke. Some texts claim that Jesus will return soon (Luke 21:25–33), but others imply a delay before his return (Luke 12:35–48). Indeed, the parable of the poor widow and the unjust judge has both themes (Luke 18:1–8). The Lord promises to give justice *soon* to believers who are oppressed; he won't delay on their behalf. And yet the parable ends with a question about whether the Son of Man will find faith on earth when he returns. There would be no question about the Son of Man finding people of faith if he came soon; in that case, there would be hardly time to lose one's faith. For those living on earth, Jesus's return seems agonizingly long, so long that they are tempted to lose heart and

50 See Jörg Frey, "Was erwartet die Johannesapokalypse? Zur Eschatologie des letzten Buchs der Bibel," in *Die Johannesapokalypse: Kontexte—Konzepte—Rezeption*, ed. Jörg Frey, James A. Kelhoffer, and Franz Tóth, WUNT 287 (Tübingen: Mohr Siebeck, 2012), 496.

give up. The paradox of the parable, the tension in the parable, is not relieved. Jesus will come soon, and yet to those on earth, it seems that his coming is delayed.

These two brief examples—and we could add here the reflections in 2 Peter 3:8–10—suggest that we should not interpret the promise that Jesus will come soon simplistically. There is a thickness and subtlety and depth to the promise, which fits with the slow progress that attended the fulfillment of God's promises from the outset. We think of how long, for instance, it took Abraham and Sarah to have a son, and the promises made to Israel were not fulfilled quickly. The promise of Jesus's coming is misappropriated if it encourages human calculation. Here the words of 2 Peter 3 and Luke 18 ring true; what seems like a long time to us is not a long time for God. Jesus's future coming reminds believers of every generation to be vigilant, for the promise is apt to be fulfilled in our generation and in our time. Yet there are no guarantees, and we are not given access to the eschatological clock, as if we can set up an eschatological timetable.

When Jesus returns, he will reward believers, and this reward will be the subject of a subsequent chapter. Here we are reminded that when he comes, he will reward all according to their works (Rev. 22:12). We should not miss the high Christology here, for in assessing and dispensing one's final reward, Jesus takes on divine functions.

Here Comes the Judge

The coming of Jesus is tied also to the judgment to come. The focus on judgment makes sense since Revelation was written to churches that were discriminated against, oppressed, and hated by the world. The coming of Jesus will establish justice in the world and make everything that is wrong right.

In Revelation 1:7, John merges together Daniel 7:13 and Zechariah 12:10: "Behold, he is coming with the clouds, and every eye will see him, even those who pierced him, and all tribes of the earth will wail on account of him." In Daniel 7, "one like a son of man" comes on the clouds to the Ancient of Days to receive the kingdom, while in Zechariah 12–13,

Israel will look on the one they pierced and mourn in repentance. Merging Daniel 7 with Zechariah 12 clarifies that the subject is Jesus's coming, the time when he returns to receive the kingdom, as Daniel 7 teaches. The consummation is at hand. The use of Zechariah is harder to assess. Given the context in Zechariah, it could be read as saying that Israel or the Gentiles or both repent upon seeing the one they pierced.[51] Such a reading is possible but unlikely. First, "all the tribes of the earth" (Rev. 1:7) should not be restricted to Israel since there is no evidence that the churches of Asia Minor consisted especially of Jewish Christians, and for John to focus on what happens in the land of Israel when writing to the seven churches strays from the situation his original readers faced. Second, we have seen that John often adjusts Old Testament citations, and in this case, he merges Zechariah 12:10 with Daniel 7:13 to establish a clear reference to the second coming. The mourning, in the context of Revelation, refers not to repentance but to the judgment that will come on those who disbelieve. Such a reading fits with the context of Revelation, where believers are beleaguered and persecuted by the society and government in which they reside. John reminds his readers in the first chapter of the book (cf. 1:5–6, 8, 17–18) that they will ultimately triumph. Their triumph will be realized at the second coming, when believers will be vindicated and the wicked will face judgment. John restates the same truth in a distinct way in 17:14, where he reflects on opponents and those who belong to Jesus: "They will make war on the Lamb, and the Lamb will conquer them, for he is Lord of lords and King of kings, and those with him are called and chosen and faithful."

An extended reflection on Jesus's coming is found in Revelation 19:11–21, and we are reminded that we have an apocalyptic, divine revelation since heaven is opened and the future is revealed to John (19:11).[52] A few interpreters reject any reference to the second com-

---

51 So Bauckham, *Climax of Prophecy*, 319–22. Osborne (*Revelation*, 70) and Koester (*Revelation*, 229) see judgment and salvation.

52 For the Old Testament background of Yahweh as the divine warrior, see Tremper Longman III and Daniel G. Reid, *God Is a Warrior*, SOTBT (Grand Rapids, MI: Zondervan, 1995).

ing, but the casting of the beast and the false prophet into the lake of fire shows that John is depicting the final judgment (19:20). Earlier John described the preternatural ability of the beast to recover from the wound of death and rise again (13:3), but the days when the beast exercises its influence end here. There are no second or third or fourth acts once it is thrown into the lake of fire. Furthermore, the killing of "the rest" (19:21) confirms that *all the enemies* of God are destroyed.

The coming of Christ is majestic, as he rides a brilliant and beautiful white horse (19:11). And this is not the coming of a tyrant who savagely abuses others because of his selfish will. Jesus is "Faithful and True" and wages war "in righteousness" (19:11; cf. Pss. 72:2; 96:13; 98:9; Isa. 11:4). The reference to war signifies that the Christ rides forth to punish and judge those who have resisted him. After all, the beast, the false prophet, and their cohorts have gathered together to make war against the Christ and his people (Rev. 19:19). The judgment meted out by Christ is not flawed by a partial or superficial vision (see Isa. 11:3); his eyes are "like a flame of fire" (Rev. 19:12), showing that his understanding of the hearts of people and of the whole of reality is comprehensive and complete (see 1:14).

We see the ineffable and majestic quality of his name since no one else knows his name, which means that no one is above him, nor is he subject to the control of anyone else (19:12). Knowing someone's name in the ancient world signified control over someone, which explains why the angel of the Lord refused to tell Jacob his name during their wrestling match (Gen. 32:29). Similarly, when Manoah, the father of Samson, asks the angel of the Lord his name, the angel replies, "Why do you ask my name, seeing it is wonderful?" (Judg. 13:18). At the same time, Jesus is also "The Word of God" (Rev. 19:13), echoing John 1:1 and 1:14; he is God's message to the world, the one who explains who God is to the human race (John 1:18),[53] though Revelation emphasizes a word of judgment here.[54]

---

53 See esp. Caird, *Revelation*, 244. Cf. Mounce, *Revelation*, 345–46; Beale, *Revelation*, 957–59; Osborne, *Revelation*, 683.
54 So Koester, *Revelation*, 756–57.

Some have claimed that the "robe dipped in blood" (Rev. 19:13) refers to the cleansing and atoning work of Christ, as in 7:14. Thus they read what is described here in terms of forgiveness of sins instead of judgment. But both the context of the present text and the Old Testament antecedents support a reference to judgment. We have already seen that the narrative concludes with the destruction of the false prophet, the beast, and those who side with them (19:20–21). Furthermore, the "sharp sword" in his mouth (19:15) signifies judgment since he uses it to strike and subdue the nations and to rule them with an iron rod, in accord with Psalm 2:9. It is clear that John is describing judgment since the nations opposing Christ will be trampled in "the winepress of the fury of the wrath of God the Almighty" (Rev. 19:15). We have already seen in 14:17–20 that the treading of the winepress signifies God's judgment (cf. Joel 3:13).

Furthermore, the phrase "a robe dipped in blood" itself conveys judgment.[55] The trampling of the winepress that leads to garments spattered with blood echoes Isaiah 63:1–6, where Yahweh's clothing is stained with blood from treading the winepress alone. He does so on his day of "vengeance" (Isa. 63:4), as he says,

> I trampled down the peoples in my anger;
> I made them drunk in my wrath,
> and I poured out their lifeblood on the earth. (Isa. 63:6)

The Isaianic reference confirms that judgment rather than salvation is in view. There is a sense in which Isaiah also refers to salvation and redemption (Isa. 63:1, 4), but we must understand what he is saying precisely: the judgment and destruction of the wicked spell redemption, relief, and salvation for the righteous. The destruction of the beast and its sidekick means that the righteous are delivered from evil forces that persecuted them. Thus the righteous are saved and delivered because the wicked who persecuted them are judged and destroyed.

---

55 So Tabb, *All Things New*, 58.

Another indication that the final judgment is at hand is the allusion to Ezekiel 39:4 and 39:17–20 in Revelation 19:17–18. Ezekiel 38–39 relates the destruction of Gog and Magog and their associates when they attempt to destroy Israel. The historical referents to the scene described in Ezekiel 38–39 are difficult to reconstruct, but the vagueness of the historical referents and the cosmic and apocalyptic nature of the language fit well with the final judgment. John picks up the grisly language of birds feasting on the flesh of those who oppose the people of God.

Conclusion

Those who have ears to hear must listen, and they must especially listen to the word about Jesus Christ. The Christology of the book of Revelation is astonishing: Jesus shares the same divine identity as God and is the Messiah of Israel. As the Lord and Christ, he redeems and frees his people from sin so that they are spared the terrible judgments that are coming. The judgment will be complete when Jesus returns, and the judgment will also represent the final vindication of believers.

The Testimony of the Holy Spirit

THE HOLY SPIRIT DOESN'T PLAY as central a role in Revelation as we find in the Gospel of John, but the Spirit appears more than we might pick up from a quick and casual reading of the book. Still, this chapter is brief since the Spirit isn't as prominent as the Father and the Son. It has been said that the Spirit is the "shy" member of the Trinity, and understood rightly, such a description fits, since the Spirit testifies to Jesus Christ. We see in this chapter that the Spirit points readers to Christ crucified and risen and that the Spirit is himself divine since grace and peace come from him. We shall see in the seven letters to the churches that the Spirit calls on the readers to hear what is being said to the churches, and thus there is a special responsibility to hear the message of the Spirit. The readers must not turn a deaf ear.

The Spirit of Revelation

The Spirit, according to John, is the Spirit of revelation, the Spirit who speaks the word of God. We could say, then, that John highlights the Spirit as the Spirit of prophecy. For instance, at key junctures in the book, John tells the reader that it was the Spirit who took hold of him to see his visions.[1] For instance, in Revelation 1:10, before John sees

---

1   See also here Richard Bauckham, *The Theology of the Book of Revelation*, New Testament Theology (Cambridge: Cambridge University Press, 1993), 116; Brian J. Tabb, *All Things*

the inaugural vision of the book, the stunning vision of the Son of Man (1:12–16), he tells us that he "was in the Spirit on the Lord's day" (1:10). John doesn't mean that he was walking in the Spirit instead of in the flesh but that the Spirit of prophecy was upon him as he saw the visions granted to him by God. We see that when the Spirit grasped him in chapter 1, he saw a vision of Jesus as the Son of Man in all his glory. We are not far from what we read in John 16:14, where Jesus says, "[The Spirit] will glorify me." The revelation of the Spirit shines the spotlight on Jesus Christ.

The notoriously difficult saying "The testimony of Jesus is the spirit of prophecy" (Rev. 19:10) probably fits this discussion. The word "spirit" (Gk. *pneuma*) here could very well be the word "spirit" with a small *s*, but even if it is, we likely have a case of a double meaning. The "essence" and heart of prophecy are inspired by the Holy Spirit himself, and the Spirit centers on the testimony about Jesus Christ.[2] The Spirit directs attention to Jesus Christ as the Lamb who is slain and as the Son of Man who rules the kings of the world. The book of Revelation doesn't feature the independent saving work of the Holy Spirit, for the Spirit shines a floodlight on Jesus Christ and beckons readers to pay heed to what Jesus has accomplished for the sake of his people. It is quite remarkable how the book of Revelation, like the Gospel of John, ties the work of the Spirit to Jesus Christ.

Another occasion when John is said to be "in the Spirit" is in Revelation 4:2, and again we have a reference to the prophetic Spirit. John then sees a vision in chapters 4–5 of God in his majesty on the throne and Christ in his glory as the Lion of the tribe of Judah and as the slain Lamb. The revelation of the Spirit comes at a key point in the narrative, when God and Christ are worshiped in the throne room. Once again, the Spirit directs attention not to himself but to God and his Christ. Here we see an implicit reference to the Trinity: the Father as Creator,

---

New: Revelation as Canonical Capstone, NSBT 48 (Downers Grove, IL: IVP Academic, 2019), 21.

2 So Bauckham, *Theology of Revelation*, 119; Richard Bauckham, *Climax of Prophecy: Studies on the Book of Revelation* (London: T&T Clark, 1993), 161.

the Son as Redeemer, and the Spirit as the one who bears witness to the work of the Father and the Son.

The third occasion when John is in the Spirit surfaces in 17:3, where John is "carried . . . away in the Spirit into a wilderness." Here he sees the vision of Babylon and predicts that judgment and destruction will come. The Spirit testifies that the reign of evil will be limited and that the righteous will triumph. Lady Babylon, who seems to be impregnable, will fall. We see a similar theme in 21:10: "He [the angel] then carried me away in the Spirit to a great, high mountain, and showed me the holy city Jerusalem coming down out of heaven from God." John in the Spirit sees two women: the wicked whore Babylon and the beautiful bride, the wife of the Lamb. Once again, the Spirit reveals the truth to John at a central juncture in the narrative. The future world, the Spirit reveals, belongs not to Babylon but to the bride; there is a new world coming, a new creation, a new heaven and earth. History ultimately belongs to the chaste and beautiful bride of the Lamb, to the heavenly Jerusalem instead of Rome, to the people of God instead of the clients of the beast.

In the letters to the seven churches, each letter refers to "what the Spirit says to the churches" (2:7, 11, 17, 29; 3:6, 13, 22), but at the same time, the messages in these letters are also the words of the risen Christ. We have an indication here that the words of Christ and the words of the Spirit can't be segregated from one another, as if Christ says one thing and the Spirit says another.[3] The Spirit is the Spirit of revelation, the Spirit of prophecy who declares and affirms Christ's words to the churches. We also have an indication in these letters of the Spirit's deity, for he speaks the words of God just as the Son of Man does. Nothing here suggests that the words of the Spirit are from a subordinate person, as if the Spirit occupies the same role as a prophet. Instead, the Spirit is put on the same level as the Christ in declaring the will and purposes of God to the churches. Still, the Spirit affirms what Christ declares to the churches, underscoring the authority of Jesus's words.

---

3   So also Bauckham, *Theology of Revelation*, 117.

The Spirit also speaks in 14:13, affirming that those who die in the Lord are blessed and that their labors will endure: "And I heard a voice from heaven saying, 'Write this: Blessed are the dead who die in the Lord from now on.' 'Blessed indeed,' says the Spirit, 'that they may rest from their labors, for their deeds follow them!'" The word of the Spirit confirms and strengthens what was already said by the heavenly voice, and we see the Spirit's role in revelation. The Spirit assures and comforts those who die that their perseverance and endurance will not be forgotten, that their sufferings are worth it, and that something better awaits them after this life ends.

The Spirit speaks in 22:17, along with the bride, the people of God, inviting Jesus to come or all to come to him in faith. The Spirit voices here a word of exhortation and desire. John goes on to say that those who are thirsty should come and "take the water of life without price." If the Spirit encourages people to come, perhaps the Spirit invites people to partake of himself, for in John 7:37, Jesus invites his hearers who are thirsty, saying, "Come to me and drink"; "rivers of living water" will "flow" from those who believe (John 7:38). But then we are told that Jesus was speaking of the Spirit, who would be given when Jesus was glorified (John 7:39).

The Seven Spirits

One of the most interesting references to the Spirit comes in the "grace and peace" wish in Revelation 1:4–6. We have seen that the Father is in view when grace and peace are said to come from "him who is and who was and who is to come" (1:4). And Jesus Christ is obviously also the source of grace and peace in 1:5. But what is the identity of "the seven spirits who are before his throne" (1:4), from whom also grace and peace come? Some claim that angels are in view, and this fits with the use of the plural *pneumata*, which in some instances refers to angels (Ps. 104:4 [103:4 LXX]; Heb. 1:7, 14; 1 Pet. 3:19).[4] Tobit 12:15 speaks

4   David E. Aune, *Revelation 1–5*, WBC 52A (Nashville: Thomas Nelson, 1997), 33–35; Craig R. Koester, *Revelation: A New Translation with Introduction and Commentary*, AB 38A (New Haven, CT: Yale University Press, 2014), 216, 226–27.

of seven angels standing before the Lord's glory, and in the Dead Sea Scrolls angels and spirits have the same referent (1QM 12.8–9). In Revelation John could be referring to angels, but it is more likely that the seven spirits refer here to the Holy Spirit (cf. Isa. 11:2; Zech. 4:1–6).[5] The number seven, as we have come to expect in Revelation, is symbolic, referring to the perfection of the Spirit, and thus John isn't speaking literally of seven different spirits. The most important argument for a reference to the Spirit is that grace and peace come from the seven spirits. We must say immediately that grace and peace don't come from the Spirit elsewhere in the New Testament, but a reference to angels is even more improbable since we have a prayer wish here, asking for grace and peace. There is no instance in which grace and peace are requested from angelic beings. Grace and peace come only from God, and thus the most probable referent is the Holy Spirit. Surprisingly, David Aune, who defends the idea that angels are intended, doesn't even mention the fundamental objection to his view, namely, the claim that grace and peace never come from angels or from human beings. Grace and peace are gifts of God, and thus we have a clear reference here to the Holy Spirit and also a text that confirms the Spirit's deity.

A reference to the Spirit isn't as unexpected when we see that Trinitarian formulas are found elsewhere in the New Testament (e.g., Matt. 28:19; 2 Cor. 13:14; Eph. 4:4–6; 1 Pet. 1:1–2).[6] We also see here an instance of at least implied prayer to the Holy Spirit since John asks for grace and peace from the Father, the Spirit, and Jesus Christ. Thus, the claim made by some that there is no instance of a prayer offered to the Spirit in the New Testament is falsified. If this reading of the seven spirits in Revelation 1:4 is correct, then it is likely that every reference to the seven spirits in Revelation refers to the Holy Spirit. We read in 3:1 that Jesus "has the seven spirits of God and the seven stars" (3:1). The seven stars

5   G. B. Caird, *A Commentary on the Revelation of St. John the Divine*, HNTC (New York: Harper & Row, 1966), 15; G. K. Beale, *The Book of Revelation: A Commentary on the Greek Text*, NIGTC (Grand Rapids, MI: Eerdmans, 1999), 189–90; Grant R. Osborne, *Revelation*, BECNT (Grand Rapids, MI: Baker Academic, 2002), 61, 74–75; Bauckham, *Theology of Revelation*, 110–11; Tabb, *All Things New*, 68–71.

6   Bauckham affirms the Trinitarian character of the salutation. *Theology of Revelation*, 24.

are identified as the angels of the churches (1:20). We can see again why some might think angels are in view since the seven spirits and seven stars are both possessed by Jesus. The argument, however, can also be turned the other way since two references to angels in the same verse would be redundant, and it doesn't necessarily follow that Jesus possesses the seven spirits and the seven stars in the same way. Jesus having the seven spirits expresses a common New Testament theme, which is that Jesus is the one who is filled with the Spirit and thus the one who gives the Spirit to his disciples (cf. Luke 4:1, 14, 18; Acts 2:33).

The next reference to seven spirits is in the throne-room vision in Revelation 4, which features the beauty, holiness, and majesty of God. We read in 4:5, "Before the throne were burning seven torches of fire, which are the seven spirits of God." The book of 1 Enoch tells us that beneath God's throne were "streams of flaming fire" (1 En. 14.19), but the parallel isn't close enough to inform the meaning of Revelation 4:5. The vagueness of the reference could support a number of interpretations, but the first reference in the book (1:4) is our clearest guide for interpreting the saying here. I take it, then, to refer to the Holy Spirit, and the burning torches probably designate the holiness of the Spirit, a holiness that can't tolerate any evil. In Isaiah the Lord cleanses the filth of Jerusalem "by a spirit of judgment and by a spirit of burning" (Isa. 4:4). Similarly, Malachi 3:2 warns Israel about the danger of the Lord's presence since "he is like a refiner's fire." Here the holiness of the Spirit is associated with the holiness of God himself (Rev. 4:8). Osborne argues that the Spirit who is perfect "oversee[s] and judge[s] his creation."[7] We may also have an allusion to Zechariah 4:2–7, where the lampstand with seven lamps represents the eyes of Yahweh; Zechariah stresses that the work of rebuilding the temple will be accomplished by the Spirit of God.[8]

The last reference to the seven spirits is in chapter 5, where Christ is celebrated as the Lion and the Lamb. John sees the slain Lamb standing

---

7   Osborne, *Revelation*, 231.
8   Tabb, *All Things New*, 70.

since he is also the conquering Lamb, the risen Lamb (Rev. 5:6). We are then told that this Lamb stands "with seven horns and with seven eyes, which are the seven spirits of God sent out into all the earth." Seven horns signify the infinite and almighty strength of the risen Lamb, while his seven eyes designate both his omniscience—nothing happens without his knowledge (see Zech. 4:10)—and his power to accomplish what he intends (2 Chron. 16:7–9). The seven eyes, however, are linked with the seven spirits sent throughout the world.[9] It might seem that the seven spirits can't be the Holy Spirit since they are identified with the seven eyes of Christ. On the other hand, this is probably an example of the fluidity of apocalyptic language, so that we have a both-and instead of an either-or. Indeed, the language of sending the seven spirits fits with what we find in the rest of the New Testament, which testifies that the Spirit is sent and given when Jesus is exalted (e.g., Luke 24:49; John 7:39; 14:16; 15:26; 16:7; Acts 1:4; 2:33). We see the same theme in Revelation 5: the risen Jesus sends his Spirit into the world as the exalted one, as the one who reigns.

We may also see a reference to the Spirit in Revelation 11:11–12, where "a breath of life" leads to the resurrection of the two witnesses.[10] This text seems to allude to Ezekiel 37, which both depicts God's breath as granting life to dead bones (Ezek. 37:5, 10) and makes a clear reference to the resurrection (Ezek. 37:14). The life of the age to come is ushered in by the Holy Spirit.

Conclusion

To sum up, the Spirit in the book of Revelation speaks the prophetic word; he is the Spirit of revelation. Believers must not close their ears to the words of the Spirit; they must hear and obey what the Spirit says. In particular, the Spirit testifies to Jesus Christ so that believers center their attention on Christ as the crucified and risen one. The Spirit works not independently of the Christ but in conjunction with him.

---

9   See Bauckham, *Theology of Revelation*, 112–13; Bauckham, *Climax of Prophecy*, 164; Beale, *Revelation*, 355; Osborne, *Revelation*, 257.

10 See Osborne, *Revelation*, 430; Tabb, *All Things New*, 74–76.

We have some justification in Revelation for identifying the Spirit as the "shy" member of the Trinity, as others have said, since the Spirit doesn't draw attention to himself. The Spirit is sent into the world after Jesus has been crucified, raised, and exalted. At the same time, the Spirit clearly shares the divine identity since grace and peace come from him, since he speaks the word of God and Christ, and since he is the Spirit of holiness.

6

The Promise of Blessing and the New Creation

IN THIS CHAPTER WE CONSIDER the final reward for believers, focusing on the blessedness promised to them and the promise of the new creation. If believers truly hear and perceive the reward that is guaranteed to them, they will continue to cling to Christ and will not forsake the gospel. But if they are deaf to the reward, if they forget about the great blessings that will be theirs, they are in danger of listening to the dragon instead of the Lamb.

The New Jerusalem and the New Temple

John in Revelation wants readers to keep their minds and hearts directed toward the future, reminding them of the world to come, of the new creation. The focus on the new creation is especially prominent in Revelation 21–22. Here we find the consummation of all things, and John sees "a new heaven and a new earth" (Rev. 21:1; cf. Isa. 65:17; 66:22; 2 Pet. 3:13), where the former world has passed away, including the sea, which symbolizes the chaos, disorder, and futility of the present world (Rev. 21:1). Remarkably, the new creation is also pictured as a city, as the "new Jerusalem" (21:2). The city is transcendent—God brings it from heaven itself. We also find in Hebrews the expectation of a heavenly city that awaits the redeemed (Heb. 11:16). Hebrews

12:22 speaks of "Mount Zion," the "city" of "the heavenly Jerusalem." Similarly, Paul contrasts the earthly Jerusalem with the transcendent Jerusalem, "the Jerusalem above" (Gal. 4:25–26).

John draws here on Isaiah 62, which anticipates a future splendor and glory for Jerusalem when the city will luxuriate in the goodness that God will bestow on her. Even more interesting is the connection with Isaiah 65, where Yahweh promises to "create new heavens / and a new earth" (Isa. 65:17), but the new world coming is portrayed as a city as well, for in the next verse, the Lord promises, "I will create Jerusalem to be a joy" (Isa. 65:18), and Israel is comforted with the assurance that God "will rejoice in Jerusalem" (Isa. 65:19). As a consequence, the people should "rejoice" over Jerusalem since the Lord will fulfill what he has promised regarding the city (Isa. 66:10). Joel looks forward to the day when Yahweh, "who dwells in Zion," will make Jerusalem holy (Joel 3:17), and then Jerusalem will be inhabited forever (Joel 3:20). Zechariah prophesies that a day will come when people from all nations will travel to Jerusalem to worship the Lord (Zech. 14:17).

The merging together of the new creation and the new Jerusalem in John, which we have already seen in Isaiah 65–66, shows that the eschatological promises to Jerusalem are no longer localized, but the entire new creation is designated the new Jerusalem. As G. K. Beale has argued, the Lord dwells in the holy city, the entire universe, as his temple.[1] We are not surprised, then, that John goes on to say in Revelation 21:3, "Behold, the dwelling place of God is with man. He will dwell with them, and they will be his people, and God himself will be with them as their God." Now temple and covenant language are applied to the new creation, to the new Jerusalem. What makes the new Jerusalem—the new universe—so enchanting, so delightful, so satisfying and enthralling is God's presence with his people. What was anticipated in God's covenant relationship with human beings is now a consummated reality. Even though John describes the new Jerusalem in some detail, as we shall

---

1   G. K. Beale, *The Temple and the Church's Mission: A Biblical Theology of the Dwelling Place of God*, NSBT 17 (Downers Grove, IL: InterVarsity Press, 2004).

see, we don't have a concrete sense of the nature of life in the new order coming. What stands out is that "the throne of God and of the Lamb will be in [the city]" (22:3). The greatest promise and hope is the beatific vision, for John assures his readers that "they will see his face" (22:4).

Still, John writes at some length on "the holy city Jerusalem coming down out of heaven from God" (21:10). It is fascinating that John "in the Spirit" was carried to "a great, high mountain" (21:10). We have a clear allusion here to Ezekiel 40:1–2, where Ezekiel is placed "on a very high mountain," and he sees a structure like a city, though the next eight chapters in Ezekiel focus on the temple and regulations regarding its rebuilding. As already mentioned, we are being told in figurative language about the final fulfillment of Ezekiel's vision of the temple. We see clearly from the way John appropriates Ezekiel in Revelation that what Ezekiel says about the temple is fulfilled in the heavenly Jerusalem, the new creation, the entire universe. John follows this up with the claim that God's glory fills the new Jerusalem and that its radiance and beauty are like a precious stone (Rev. 21:11). We see again an allusion both to Ezekiel, where the glory of God returns to the temple (Ezek. 43:2–5), and to the promise of Isaiah that God's glory will shine again in Israel (Isa. 60:1, 19).

The city is enclosed and protected with "a great, high wall" (Rev. 21:12). The language is clearly symbolic, for a high and impregnable wall in the ancient world would protect cities from enemies, but today such a city could be bombed to smithereens from above. Perhaps some will reject the last argument as anachronistic, but John also tells us that the gates of the city "will never be shut by day—and there will be no night there" (21:25). There is no need for a high and massive wall if the gates of the city are perpetually left open! By leaving the gates open, a city invites attack. Both pictures, of course, the high wall and the open gates, teach the same lesson in apocalyptic and figurative language: the people of God are entirely safe in the new creation.[2] Nothing can harm them there; saying that there is no night is not an astronomical

---

2   So Grant R. Osborne, *Revelation*, BECNT (Grand Rapids, MI: Baker Academic, 2002), 764.

observation but a way of saying that evil doesn't exist in the new world that is coming.

Similarly, saying that the wall is 144 cubits is also symbolic since the number 144 is gained by multiplying 12 x 12 (21:17), and the number twelve is certainly used symbolically in Revelation. Another indication of the symbolism present here is the appeal to angelic measurement in 21:17. Such an explanation scarcely helps readers since we don't know how angels measure. It will not do to say that John's point is that angels measure in the same way as human beings, because such a prosaic comment adds nothing to our understanding.[3] John mentions angelic measurements so that readers will realize that he writes symbolically. The 144 cubits could refer to the height or thickness of the wall, but since we have already been told that the wall is high (21:12), it probably designates its thickness. The wall would be 216 feet thick, which is impossibly dense (showing again the symbolism present here), and again we face the question about the point of having such a thick wall if the gates are left open. John conveys again to the reader in figurative terms the security and safety of the city.

We find the same idea of safety in the measurement of the city, its gates, and its walls (21:15). Measuring designates protection, as in the measuring of the temple, the altar, and the worshipers in 11:1 or, as discussed above, in the measurement of the wall in 144 cubits (21:17). The detailed measurements for the temple area in Ezekiel 40–42 (cf. Ezek. 48:16, 30, 33) signify that the temple will be built again, that it won't be destroyed, and that the temple will prosper. John, of course, doesn't understand the Ezekielian temple literally, seeing instead its fulfillment in the new creation since there is no temple in the world to come. In Zechariah 2:1–5, the measuring of the city of Jerusalem signifies its prosperity and protection. We see a remarkable parallel with Revelation 21:25, where the gates never close, in Zechariah 2:4, where the city Jerusalem is "inhabited as villages without walls" because of

---

3   Against Osborne, *Revelation*, 754. Rightly, G. K. Beale, *The Book of Revelation: A Commentary on the Greek Text*, NIGTC (Grand Rapids, MI: Eerdmans, 1999), 1077; Craig R. Koester, *Revelation: A New Translation with Introduction and Commentary*, AB 38A (New Haven, CT: Yale University Press, 2014), 817.

its burgeoning population (Zech. 2:4). Its protection comes from the Lord, and he affirms in the next verse, "I will be to her a wall of fire all around, declares the Lord, and I will be the glory in her midst" (Zech. 2:5). We see here how John appropriates and understands Zechariah's promises of prosperity for Jerusalem, seeing its fulfillment in the new creation, the heavenly Jerusalem. At the same time, we are struck by the remarkable emphasis on safety, security, and protection in the vision. Believers will not be motivated to endure persecution and to resist assimilation and compromise unless they are full of assurance that a better world is coming, that their suffering will not last forever.

The city has twelve gates and twelve foundations, with angels at the gates (certainly signifying protection). The names of the twelve tribes are written on the gates, and the twelve apostles are the foundation of the gates (Rev. 21:12–14). We see another allusion to the Ezekielian temple, which features twelve gates named after Israel's tribes (Ezek. 48:30–35). In the new creation, there is one people of God based on the foundation of the apostolic gospel (Eph. 2:20), and the true people of God, the true Israel, which fulfills the hopes and promises given to Israel, is found in the church of Jesus Christ. At the same time, we see that the city is not only a city but, in light of Ezekiel, also a new temple, and it is striking that the last words in the book of Ezekiel are "The LORD Is There" (Ezek. 48:35). The city in Ezekiel, which is also a temple, is marked by the presence of God. The same truth is conveyed another way in Revelation. The city is a perfect square, and "its length and width and height are equal" (Rev. 21:16). John alludes to the most holy place in the temple, where "the interior of the sanctuary [is] thirty feet long, thirty feet wide, and thirty feet high" (1 Kings 6:20 CSB). The sanctuary where God specially dwells is also a perfect square, and so once again, we see that the city is God's sanctuary and that what makes the city distinctive is not its brilliant beauty but God's presence.[4] Incidentally, we have another indication that the language is symbolic, for the city would be 1,400 to 1,500 miles in

---

4   Cf. Mathias Rissi, *The Future of the World: An Exegetical Study of Revelation 19.11–22.15*, SBT, 2nd ser., vol. 23 (Naperville, IL: A R. Allenson, 1966), 62.

all three directions if the text is taken literally, which is impossibly large. Versions that translate the number literally, such as the NET ("fourteen hundred miles"), fail to see the symbolic significance in the ESV's literal rendering "12,000 stadia" (Rev. 21:16). We have the apocalyptic use of numbers where 12 x 1,000 symbolizes not the exact dimensions of the city but its transcendence. We should also infer from the large number that the city represents the entire universe, the whole of the new creation.

John also depicts the intense beauty of the city: "Its radiance [was] like a most rare jewel, like a jasper, clear as crystal" (21:11). The wall in the city was made of jasper stone, and "the city was pure gold, like clear glass" (21:18). The foundations of the city's walls were adorned with twelve different kinds of jewels (21:19–20). We are reminded of the twelve stones in the high priest's breastpiece (Ex. 28:15–21), where the twelve stones represent the twelve Israelite tribes. We also have an allusion to Isaiah 54:11–12, where the Lord comforts Jerusalem:

> Behold, I will set your stones in antimony,
>   and lay your foundations with sapphires.
> I will make your pinnacles of agate,
>   your gate of carbuncles,
>   and all your wall of precious stones.

Ezekiel describes the beauty of Eden in similar terms:

> You were in Eden, the garden of God;
>   every precious stone was your covering,
> sardius, topaz, and diamond,
>   beryl, onyx, and jasper,
> sapphire, emerald, and carbuncle;
>   and crafted in gold were your settings
>   and your engravings. (Ezek. 28:13)

We should not press each jewel for particular symbolic significance, nor should we read the description literally. John describes the stunning and gleaming and unparalleled beauty of the city. It will be as dazzling and entrancing as life in Eden, but at the same time, the stones point to the new Jerusalem being a temple where the Lord dwells.[5]

The allusions to the Ezekielian temple might lead some to conclude that there will be a literal temple in the new creation, but John clarifies that there is no temple, because the Lord and the Lamb are the temple (Rev. 21:22), and they, rather than the sun or the moon, illumine the city (21:23). Questions are raised about the nature of the new creation from this description. Is it radically different from the present created order (cf. Rom. 8:18–25) or from the present world order? It is difficult to be sure since we are not given much information about the new heavens and new earth. We can safely say that there is both continuity and discontinuity between the present creation and the future world, but the extent of continuity and discontinuity is difficult to determine, given the paucity of discussion. Perhaps the language of the Lord and the Lamb being light is symbolic, as when we are told that "night will be no more" (Rev. 22:5). The point is that evil will be erased forever. On this scenario, the references to night and light are symbolic and don't grant us any information about the nature of the new creation.

We are also told that nations will walk by the light of God Almighty and the Lamb, and what is glorious and beautiful among the nations will be brought into the heavenly city (21:24, 26). The notion of light coming and shining on the people, a light and glory that is from the Lord, stems from Isaiah 60:1. Darkness will envelop the wicked, but the Lord's light and glory will shine on his people (Isa. 60:2). As a result,

Nations shall come to your light,
　　and kings to the brightness of your rising. (Isa. 60:3)

Furthermore, the "wealth of the nations will come to you" (Isa. 60:5). We must again recognize the apocalyptic character of the language, for

5　Richard Bauckham, *The Theology of the Book of Revelation*, New Testament Theology (Cambridge: Cambridge University Press, 1993), 134.

we should not envision nations literally bringing in what is glorious and beautiful into the new creation. In the same way, the tree of life that has leaves for the "healing of the nations" should not be taken literally (Rev. 22:2). The tree of life, of course, is picked up from the early chapters of Genesis (Gen. 2:9), and the notion that the leaves of the tree will heal stems from Ezekiel 47:12, which is part of Ezekiel's description of the new temple. John picks it up to signify that no one in the new creation gets sick and stands in need of healing; the tree of life and its healing properties point to the perfect shalom and health present in the new Jerusalem. Similarly, the wealth and glory of the nations indicate that everything that is beautiful in the present world, everything that leads to human flourishing and well-being, and everything that brings joy will be in the new creation. John doesn't linger to give details, but there is no place for looking back longingly to the old creation as if it contains beauty and loveliness that will be missing in the world to come.

In the same way, "the river of the water of life," which flowed from God's throne and the Lamb, runs in "the middle of the street of the city" (Rev. 22:1–2). We have an echo here of the river flowing out of Eden (Gen. 2:10), and we see again the contribution of Ezekiel 47, where we read the fascinating account of a river that begins with a trickle from under the threshold of the temple, and as Ezekiel travels east, the stream increases in volume until it becomes a rushing river (Ezek. 47:1–5). The river enlivens the Dead Sea and produces life wherever it flows (Ezek. 47:6–12). In Zechariah we see that waters will stream out of Jerusalem, half to the Dead Sea and half to the Mediterranean Sea (Zech. 14:8). It is quite clear that the descriptions in both Ezekiel and Zechariah are figurative. Rivers never grow in volume and strength if tributaries are not feeding into them, nor do rivers flow both east and west. We should envision neither a literal tree of life nor a river flowing from under the temple, but the image of a river points to refreshment, joy, and fulfillment in the new world. Nothing unclean or defiling or evil is in the city (Rev. 21:27; cf. 21:8) because God is "making all things new" (21:5). No more tears, no more death, and no more pain exist since the old creation has "passed away" (21:4).

It is fascinating to discover that the new-creation promises are present already in 7:15–17, which adds weight to the idea that Revelation should not be read as a linear, chronological narrative. Those who are sealed (7:4–8), that is, the uncountable multitude whose clothing was washed in the Lamb's blood (7:9–14), are promised that they will inherit the new creation. Serving God in his temple points forward to God's presence with his people in the new creation (7:15), even though there is no temple in the new creation (21:22), for the temple signifies that the Lord dwells with them (Ezek. 37:27; Rev. 21:3). If we have doubts about whether 7:15–17 refers to the new creation, 7:16–17 removes them. For those who have come out of the great tribulation, which is all believers, are free from hunger, thirst, and the scorching heat of the sun (7:16). The allusion is to Isaiah 49:10, where God promises to provide for Israel when they return from exile, but John lifts the promises to a higher key, to the ultimate return from exile, to the return to Eden. In the new creation, the Lamb will shepherd the flock and refresh them with "springs of living water" (Rev. 7:17). This is the same quenching of thirst promised in 21:6. The decisive words are the promise that "God will wipe away every tear from their eyes" (7:17), which is repeated virtually word for word in 21:4, confirming that the new creation is in view in 7:17, because tears will continue as long as the present evil age continues.

People and Place

One final issue should be addressed. Is the reference to the new creation tied exclusively to a place, or does it also include a people? The question arises because of texts like Revelation 21:2 and 21:9–10. John declares in 21:2, "I saw the holy city, new Jerusalem, coming down out of heaven from God, prepared as a bride adorned for her husband." And we read in 21:9–10,

> Then came one of the seven angels who had the seven bowls full of the seven last plagues and spoke to me, saying, "Come, I will show you the Bride, the wife of the Lamb." And he carried me away in

the Spirit to a great, high mountain, and showed me the holy city Jerusalem coming down out of heaven from God.

These texts are fascinating, especially 21:9–10, because John is *told* about a bride and *sees* a city. As we have seen, John spends almost all his time describing the dimensions and nature of the city, the heavenly Jerusalem. So should we follow what we have seen earlier about the 144,000 and the uncountable multitude and about the Lion and the Lamb? In both those instances, what John heard and what he saw was the *same entity* from two different perspectives. The referent was the same, but it was described from two different angles. We could say, as Robert Gundry argues, that the heavenly Jerusalem is as beautiful and lovely as a bride, and we have a people described here, not a place.[6]

Certainly, a people is in view since the marriage of the Lamb to his bride becomes a reality at the consummation (19:7). Indeed, a particular blessedness is pronounced on those invited to "the marriage supper of the Lamb" (19:9). It seems reductionistic to conclude, with the detailed descriptions of the city and the many allusions to a new temple, that the city is nothing more than the bride. The remarkable descriptions of the city suggest that the city should not be collapsed into the bride. Perhaps the best solution, then, is found in opting for a both-and answer. The eschatological consummation has to do with a people and a place.[7] We look forward to the marriage supper of the Lamb and the dawn of the new creation, to a wedding and to a city.

Conclusion

We have seen in this book that believers face fearsome opponents: the devil, the two beasts, and Babylon in all its glory. In the midst of cosmic conflict, God summons believers to persevere and endure, to be faithful until the end, and to resist compromise and assimilation

---

6   Robert H. Gundry, "The New Jerusalem: People as Place, Not Place for People," *NovT* 29, no. 3 (1987): 254–64.

7   See the discussion in Bauckham, *Theology of Revelation*, 132–40. Cf. Osborne, *Revelation*, 733.

with the world. The resources for such perseverance come from God himself, from the Father, the Son, and the Spirit. The evil present in the world will not triumph since God rules as the sovereign Creator over all. As the ever Holy One, he will judge evil and make everything right in the world. Believers themselves were once aligned with evil, but they have now been redeemed, released, and freed by the blood of Christ. Jesus Christ has defeated Satan and cast him out of heaven, and there is no place for accusations against believers. Jesus saves his people as the messianic King and as one who shares God's very identity. The Spirit testifies to the message communicated in Revelation, summoning readers to hear what he says. The church must not close its ears but must hear the Spirit's testimony to what God has done in Jesus Christ. A great and final reward awaits those who belong to God and Christ; all the suffering they endure for Christ's sake will be worth it. John describes this reward in symbolic language since the new creation transcends our present capacity to understand it. He depicts the reward to come as a marriage, the marriage of the people of God as a bride to the Lamb. He also portrays it as a transformed city, a new and purified Jerusalem, a city that is safe and secure and indescribably beautiful. At the same time, he represents the city as a temple, showing that God dwells in it. The most wonderful thing about the city is God's presence, seeing God's face, enjoying fellowship with him.

Reigning with Christ for
One Thousand Years

THIS CHAPTER IS A KIND of appendix since the main theological
truths of the book have been treated in previous chapters. Still, the
great interest in the millennium warrants a brief discussion. One
of the most difficult issues in Revelation centers on the meaning of
Revelation 20, where the saints are promised that they will reign with
Christ for one thousand years. Three views have attracted believers
in history: postmillennialism, premillennialism, and amillennialism.[1]
The issue of the millennium isn't of central importance for the Christian faith or for interpreting Revelation.[2] Disputes over the meaning
of the thousand-year reign have arisen because this is the only place

---

1   For helpful discussions of the various options, see Robert G. Clouse, ed., *The Meaning
of the Millennium: Four Views* (Downers Grove, IL: InterVarsity Press, 1977); Darrell L.
Bock, ed., *Three Views on the Millennium and Beyond* (Grand Rapids, MI: Zondervan,
1999).

2   For an intriguing and distinctive view, see J. Webb Mealy, *After the Thousand Years:
Resurrection and Judgment in Revelation 20*, JSNTSup 70 (Sheffield: Sheffield Academic
Press, 1992). For critiques of Mealy, see Greg K. Beale, "Review Article: J. W. Mealy *After
the Thousand Years*," *EvQ* 66, no. 3 (1994): 229–49; Charles E. Hill, review of *After the
Thousand Years*, by J. Webb Mealy, *JBL* 114, no. 1 (1995): 169–72. Hill notes that Mealy's
interpretation, although ingenious in many respects, is quite complex and requires an
amazingly astute reader, and the very complexity of the proffered interpretation renders
it improbable.

in the Scriptures where a millennial reign is explicitly taught. Actually, disputes over the millennium began very early. Papias, Justin
Martyr, Tertullian, Victorinus, and Irenaeus, among others, were
clearly premillennial, but Charles Hill has argued that there were early
versions of amillennialism as well,[3] though there is no direct mention
of the millennium in the sources Hill cites. Dogmatic opinions about
the importance of the millennium have bedeviled the church in the
last two hundred years, and some have mistakenly teetered close to
seeing it as a matter of critical orthodoxy. Still, strong feelings are
hardly new. When Eusebius discussed the premillennial view of Papias, he mockingly dismissed his view, remarking that Papias was a
person of limited intelligence.[4] Thus, put-downs of those who hold
alternative views have a long history.

Postmillenialism

Postmillennialists believe that Christ will come after a time of prosperity and blessing on earth. The number *one thousand* is symbolic,
and the millennium may have begun at Christ's resurrection, or
perhaps it is inaugurated at some unspecified time in history. In the
American experience, postmillennialism has been associated with
manifest destiny, with a secular conception that life will get better
and better. Evangelical postmillennialists, however, reject such a notion, arguing that the world is transformed by the proclamation of
the gospel of Christ, not through some worldly or secular program.
Thus, the claim that postmillennialism necessarily endorses a political or liberal view of social progress is mistaken. In the history of
interpretation, postmillennialism was especially promulgated by the
Puritans, and they definitely did not believe that a political program
would transform society.[5]

3   Charles E. Hill, *Regnum Caelorum: Patterns of Millennial Thought in Early Christianity*,
    2nd ed. (Grand Rapids, MI: Eerdmans, 2001).
4   Eusebius, *Ecclesiastical History*, trans. Kirsopp Lake, LCL 153, 265 (Cambridge, MA:
    Harvard University Press, 1992–1994), 3.39.12–13.
5   See Iain H. Murray, *The Puritan Hope: Revival and the Interpretation of Prophecy* (Carlisle,
    PA: Banner of Truth, 1971).

My purpose isn't to explain fully the postmillennial viewpoint but to focus on its reading of Revelation. For postmillennialists it is crucial to say that Revelation 19:11–21 isn't about the future coming of Christ but about the progress of the gospel in the world. The sword coming from his mouth (19:15) represents not a word of judgment but the message of the gospel that triumphs over enemies. The war (19:11) and armies (19:14) represent the truth that the gospel conquers all opponents, and slowly but surely, God vanquishes his enemies and transforms society through gospel witness. The Lord Jesus Christ removes opponents of the gospel as he rides in triumph throughout the world. In one sense, postmillennialists are similar to premillennialists, in that they envision the transformation of *this* world, of life on earth, though they are distinguished from premillennialists in that they see the transformation of the world as taking place *before* Christ returns. In another sense, postmillennialists are similar to amillennialists in that they see the rapture, the return of Christ, the final judgment, and the arrival of the new creation as occurring at the same time.

In the postmillennial scheme, the binding of Satan in the abyss begins either at the cross and resurrection or at an unspecified point in history. In any case, the binding of Satan will become progressively clearer as the gospel advances in the world. Some postmillennialists take the first resurrection to be spiritual in the same way as amillennialists, and others understand it to refer to the spirit of the martyrs and the revival of the church. Postmillennialists see a short period of evil breaking out in the world before Christ returns.

I have described postmillennialism only briefly since few advocate this reading today. The most significant problem for postmillennialism in the book of Revelation is the interpretation it proposes for Revelation 19:11–21. According to postmillennialism, this passage does not and cannot refer to the second coming of Christ. I have argued previously, however, that the passage clearly refers to the second coming and the final judgment. If that claim holds, then regardless of what postmillennialists make of Revelation 20, the postmillennial view fails.

Premillennialism

We turn next to premillennialism, which comes in two varieties today, historic premillennialism and dispensational premillennialism. Historic premillennialism is so named because it harks back to some of the earliest interpreters in the church, including Papias, Justin Martyr, Irenaeus, and others. Dispensational premillennialism, on the other hand, has its roots in the nineteenth century and the teachings of John Nelson Darby. Dispensational premillennialism holds that there will be a secret rapture seven years before the millennium begins. Space is lacking here to discuss the view of the rapture defended by premillennialists, and many wonderful believers defend this position. Still, Revelation doesn't mention the rapture, and I would argue, though the issue cannot be adjudicated in this volume, that the evidence for a pretribulation rapture is unconvincing.[6] The purpose here is to discuss premillennialism since both dispensational and historic premillennialists argue that Christ will return before the millennium and reign for one thousand years on the earth. Most premillennialists maintain that the one thousand years is a literal period, but some premillennialists argue that the number is symbolic, representing a significant period when Christ reigns on earth.

The premillennial view has a number of strengths, and many interpreters defend this understanding of Revelation 20.[7] Some wonder about the purpose of the one-thousand-year reign of Christ on earth, but premillennialists argue that the rule of the Messiah in history fulfills the promises given to Abraham and to David and his offspring about the rule of a Davidic king *on earth*. Some also point out that the

6   See Douglas J. Moo, "The Case for the Posttribulation Rapture Position," in *The Rapture: Pre-, Mid-, or Post-Tribulational?* (Grand Rapids, MI: Zondervan, 1984), 171–211.

7   An excellent defense of premillennialism is presented by Matt Waymeyer, *Amillennialism and the Age to Come: A Premillennial Critique of the Two-Age Model* (The Woodlands, TX: Kress Biblical Resources, 2016). See also Harold W. Hoehner, "Evidence from Revelation 20," in *A Case for Premillennialism: A New Consensus*, ed. Donald K. Campbell and Jeffrey L. Townsend (Chicago: Moody Press, 1992), 235–62; Craig L. Blomberg and Sung Wook Chung, eds., *A Case for Historic Premillennialism: An Alternative to "Left Behind" Eschatology* (Grand Rapids, MI: Baker Academic, 2009).

depth of human evil is revealed since humanity rebels near the end of the millennium, even though human beings have lived in a virtual paradise, showing in a new way the need for redemption. The following arguments from Revelation 20 support a premillennial interpretation.

First, the words "then I saw" (20:1) indicate that the vision that follows takes place *after* the coming of Christ in 19:11–21. Christ comes in 19:11–21, and then the one-thousand-year reign begins in chapter 20. The two events should not be merged together, and this is confirmed by 20:10, for the devil is thrown into "the lake of fire that burns with sulfur," where "the beast and the false prophet" *were* cast in the battle of 19:11–21. Revelation 20 says nothing about the beast and false prophet, for they were judged at the second coming, and the devil is judged at the end of the millennium.

Second, an angel descends from heaven, seizes Satan, and confines him with a great chain to the abyss for a thousand years (20:1–3). The millennium has to be after the second coming of Christ (19:11–21) because the devil is "the ruler of this world" (John 12:31; 16:11) and "the god of this world" (2 Cor. 4:4) and because "the whole world lies in the power of the evil one" (1 John 5:19). But the devil's rule ends when he is confined to the abyss for one thousand years. Furthermore, John says that during the one thousand years, except for a short interval at the end, the devil can't deceive the nations since he is enclosed in the abyss (Rev. 20:3). On the other hand, when the devil is active—that is, when he is cast down to the earth—he is "the deceiver of the whole world" (12:9). The casting to the earth in 12:9 is distinguished from being confined to the abyss in 20:3 because when Satan is on earth, he deceives the world, but when he is shut up in the abyss, he has no ability to deceive the world. Premillennialists also point out that it makes little sense to say that Satan is prevented from deceiving the nations in the present era since it is quite obvious that the world is still being deceived by his stratagems.

Third, Revelation 20:4 says that the souls that were put to death "came to life and reigned with Christ for a thousand years." The verb "came to life" (Gk. *ezēsan*) refers to their physical resurrection, and this makes

sense since the souls that were dead come to life. The same verb refers
to Christ's resurrection in 2:8, where we are told that he "died and came
to life" (Gk. *ezēsen*). What makes this argument even more powerful is
the statement that "the rest of the dead did not come to life [Gk. *ezēsan*]
until the thousand years were ended" (20:5). Amillennialists agree that
"the rest of the dead" refers to unbelievers and that their coming to
life (which is the same verb used in 20:4 of the martyrs coming to life)
refers to the resurrection of unbelievers when the millennium is over.
But if the verb "came to life" (Gk. *ezēsan*) refers the second time to a
physical resurrection, it almost surely has the same meaning the first
time as well. And there is even more evidence to support this view.
The coming to life of the martyrs is described as "the first resurrection"
(20:5–6), and as N. T. Wright claims in his book on the resurrection,
the word "resurrection" (Gk. *anastasis*) in every instance in the New
Testament except here refers to the physical resurrection.[8] Thus we
have good reasons to think that the physical resurrection is intended
here as well. J. Ramsey Michaels makes another observation that is
pertinent. If physical resurrection is not promised here, we have no
text in Revelation that promises the resurrection of believers, which
seems quite strange in a book that heralds the final hope of believers.[9]

Fourth, the duration of the saints' reign points to a physical resurrection since we are told twice that the martyrs will reign "for a thousand
years" (20:4, 6). The accusative phrase "a thousand years" (Gk. *chilia
etē*) refers to the duration of the saints' rule, but it is difficult to see
how this fits with an amillennial or postmillennial reading since many
believers reign not for the *entire millennium* but only at death or when
they are regenerated. Premillennialists, however, say that the phrase

---

8   N. T. Wright, *The Resurrection of the Son of God*, Christian Origins and the Question of
     God 3 (Minneapolis: Fortress, 2003), passim. See, e.g., 473–75, where he states, "'Res-
     urrection' did not mean that someone possessed 'a heavenly and exalted status'; when
     predicated of Jesus, it did not mean his 'perceived presence' in the ongoing church. Nor,
     if we are thinking historically, could it have meant 'the passage of the human Jesus into
     the power of God.' It meant bodily resurrection; and that is what the early Christians
     affirmed." But he argues for an exception in Rev. 20.
9   J. Ramsey Michaels, "The First Resurrection: A Response," *WTJ* 39, no. 1 (1976): 100–109.

"a thousand years" is much more naturally understood to refer to the entire period of the millennium.

Fifth, premillennialists point to Old Testament texts that anticipate the rule of God's people—more specifically, Israel—on earth, and they conclude that these prophecies are fulfilled in the millennium. Many texts are included here, such as Isaiah 60; 62; and 65:17–25. Others that are often adduced are Ezekiel 36–39 and Ezekiel 40–48, the description of the new temple. Many premillennialists argue that the millennium fulfills the prophecies in Jeremiah 30–33 or Zechariah 9–14, and a number of other texts could be cited as well.

Sixth, two Old Testament texts in particular are used to support a premillennial interpretation. We read in Isaiah 24:21–23,

> On that day the LORD will punish
>> the host of heaven, in heaven,
>> and the kings of the earth, on the earth.
> They will be gathered together
>> as prisoners in a pit;
> they will be shut up in a prison,
>> and after many days they will be punished.
> Then the moon will be confounded
>> and the sun ashamed,
> for the LORD of hosts reigns
>> on Mount Zion and in Jerusalem,
> and his glory will be before his elders.

The punishment of the army and kings represents the second coming (Rev. 19:11–21), but the confining to the dungeon for many days constitutes the millennial period, and the final punishment doesn't occur for "many days" (Isa. 24:22).

Another key text is Isaiah 65:17–25, which promises the arrival of a new heaven and a new earth. Joy will reverberate in Jerusalem, and people will build, plant, and enjoy prosperity. The "wolf and the lamb" will dwell and "graze together" without harming one another, and lions will become vegetarian. No children will die in infancy, and those who don't live a hundred years will be considered cursed. Premillennialists point out that this text must refer to the millennium, for even though life is wonderful on the earth, death still exists, and there will be no death in the new creation.

Amillennialism

A premillennial reading is quite plausible and may even be the most compelling. We have to admit that the text isn't entirely clear here, and there are good arguments for both positions. Amillennialism argues that the millennium is during the church age for the following reasons.

No other text clearly and specifically teaches premillennialism, and establishing a doctrine based on one text, especially a text that is apocalyptic in nature, is inadvisable. Amillennialism fits with the whole teaching of Scripture if the second coming, the resurrection of the dead, and the final judgment take place at the same time. In contrast, if premillennialism is correct, the judgment of the sheep and goats, described in Matthew 25:31–46, doesn't occur at the same time. The sheep enter into their final reward one thousand years before the goats are punished. Such a scenario is possible, but it seems like a strained and forced reading. Furthermore, it seems strange, on the premillennial schema, that glorified and unglorified saints live on earth together, though we must admit that strange and unforeseen things happen. Still, one wonders how unglorified people enter the millennium since Revelation 19:21 says "the rest" were killed by the sword that comes out of the Lord's mouth. The killing of the rest doesn't seem to leave room for any other human beings to enter a so-called millennial kingdom. Premillennialists offer various arguments for the entrance of some unbelieving people into the millennium, but such arguments are hard to square with Revelation 19:21.

Premillennialists often argue that the words "then I saw" (Gk. *kai eidon*) in 20:1 indicate that we have a chronological progression from Christ's second coming in chapter 19. But the argument isn't decisive, for we see the same phrase, "then I saw," in 20:4, and the vision described in 20:4–6, as all premillennialists agree, refers to the same period—the one-thousand-year reign explained in 20:1–3. Thus, the words "then I saw" don't necessarily indicate a chronological progression. Such a view needs to be established on other grounds. Also, the claim that the beast and false prophet are thrown into the lake of fire (19:20) one thousand years before Satan is cast into the lake (20:10) is disputable. Some English translations insert the word "were" in 20:10 (e.g., ESV, NRSV, RSV; cf. NIV, "had been thrown"), which implies that the beast and false prophet were thrown into hell before Satan was. In fact, however, there is no verb in the Greek text, and the verb could also be rendered "are" (see CSB, HCSB, KJV, NASB). On this reading, the beast, the false prophet, and Satan could meet their fate at the same time. In other words, the account of Satan's downfall could recapitulate the same events described in 19:11–21.

Furthermore, a good argument can be made for recapitulation in 19:11–21 and 20:1–10.[10] Both texts allude to Ezekiel 38–39. In Revelation 19, the opponents of Christ are destroyed by his word, and "all the birds [are] gorged with their flesh" (19:21). The birds consuming the flesh of human beings fulfills Ezekiel 39:4 and 39:17–20. We see another allusion to Ezekiel 38–39 in Revelation 20:8–9, where the nations come up to fight against the people of God and are called "Gog and Magog" (20:8). John is, of course, indebted to Ezekiel, who identifies the opponents of Israel as Gog and Magog (Ezek. 38:2–3, 16, 18; 39:1, 6, 11, 15). John says the opposition will be "like the sand of the sea" (Rev. 20:8), and Ezekiel says it will be "a great host" (Ezek. 38:4). According to John, Gog and Magog have come for "battle," or we could say, given the Greek, "the battle" (Gk. *ton polemon*, Rev. 20:8). And the battle here may be the same one described in Revelation 19:19, since the two

10   See R. Fowler White, "Reexamining the Evidence for Recapitulation in Rev 20:1–10," *WTJ* 51, no. 2 (1989): 319–44. See also Brian J. Tabb, *All Things New: Revelation as Canonical Capstone*, NSBT 48 (Downers Grove, IL: IVP Academic, 2019), 132–33.

passages use the exact same two words, "the battle" (Gk. *ton polemon*). Indeed, these two references may very well be another way of describing the battle of Armageddon (16:16), which is also identified as the "battle [Gk. *ton polemon*] on the great day of God the Almighty" (16:14). John informs the readers that fire from God destroys the enemies of God, Gog and Magog (20:9), and this picks up the judgment of fire from Ezekiel 38:22 and 39:6. Both Revelation 19:11–21 and 20:1–10 allude to Ezekiel 38–39, but the judgments in Ezekiel 38–39 refer to the same eschatological event. Daniel Block says that Ezekiel 38–39 has eight frames that are to be interpreted as a "literary cartoon" portraying one attack and destruction.[11] The argument here is that Ezekiel 38–39 portrays in various ways the last battle, and the different scenarios represent the end in compatible ways. Since John picks up on Ezekiel's depiction of the last battle in both Revelation 19 and 20, there are good grounds for thinking that Revelation 20 recapitulates the last battle described in Revelation 19. If that is the case, Revelation 20 doesn't depict a one-thousand-year period after the second coming. Instead, the one-thousand-year period is an alternative way of depicting life on earth and in heaven before the second coming.

Another argument supporting amillennialism is that texts that are typically thought to support premillennialism, when considered further, can be seen to support amillennialism. We will briefly consider four passages: Ezekiel 40–48; Isaiah 2:2–4; Isaiah 60; and Isaiah 65:17–25. All four of these texts are commonly presented as favoring premillennialism, but when we examine them more closely, they actually support amillennialism.

First, we reflect on Ezekiel 40–48, which describes the building of the new temple and the regulations accompanying such a rebuilding. The goal here isn't to investigate the chapters in all possible detail but to make general observations. Table 7.1 traces the allusions to Ezekiel 40–48 in Revelation.

---

11 Daniel I. Block, *The Book of Ezekiel: Chapters 25–48*, NICOT (Grand Rapids, MI: Eerdmans, 1998), 431.

Table 7.1   Ezekiel and Revelation Compared

Ezekiel		Revelation	
40:2	Vison on a mountain of a city	21:10	Vison on a mountain of the heavenly Jerusalem
40:3, 5	Measuring the wall outside the temple	21:15	Measuring the city
47:1	Water flowing from the temple	22:1	River flowing from the throne of God and the Lamb
47:12	Trees for healing	22:2, 14, 19	Tree of life for healing
48:16–17	Measurement of the city	21:16–17	Dimension of the city and measurement of the wall
48:30–35	Gates of the city: "The LORD Is There"	21:12–13	Gates of the city

What is striking is that every single allusion from Ezekiel 40–48 found in Revelation 21–22 describes the new heavens and new earth, and not a single allusion from Ezekiel 40–48 exists in the millennial passage (Rev. 20). I conclude from this that Ezekiel 40–48 is fulfilled in the new heavens and new earth (Rev. 21–22), not in the millennium (Rev. 20).

It does not follow from this that a new temple will be in the new heavens and new earth, since John specifically tells us that there will be no temple in the new creation because the Lord himself and the Lamb are the temple (21:22). Ezekiel uses the imagery and language of his day when he describes the temple, but the fulfillment doesn't occur in a literal way. Some might argue from Ezekiel 40–48 that the temple will be rebuilt in the millennium as a precursor to what will exist in the new heavens and new earth. Such a scenario has problems. First, the teaching in the epistle to the Hebrews, where Christ is the final and definitive sacrifice, makes it impossible to believe that the Old Testament sacrifices described in Ezekiel 40–48 will be reinstituted. Some argue that they will be reintroduced as a memorial of Christ's sacrifice, but we already have a memorial of Christ's sacrifice—the Lord's Supper. There is really no good explanation for why the Lord's Supper would be replaced by animal sacrifices. Second, even in Ezekiel there is no expectation that the temple described will ever be built. Ezekiel 40–48 doesn't envision the building of a literal temple, for it lacks detailed instructions to complete such a structure.[12] Block says, "The description of the temple is not presented as a blueprint for some future building to be constructed with human hands"; it describes a "spiritual reality in concrete terms."[13] Thomas Renz also argues that the new temple does not constitute the rebuilding of the old one.[14] As William J. Dumbrell similarly states, "The details are not a plan for physical rebuilding."[15] And Kalinda Rose Stevenson observes that no blueprint for building the temple exists here, for vertical dimensions are entirely lacking.[16]

The use of Ezekiel 40–48 plays an important role hermeneutically, for we see that Old Testament prophecies are clothed in the language of their time, and we need to pay attention particularly to how the New Testament understands prophecies to see how they will be fulfilled in redemptive history. Space is lacking to unpack every text, but we can see how such a hermeneutic applies to other texts that are allegedly about the millennium.

Our second example comes from Isaiah 2:2–4, which many see as a text supporting premillennialism (cf. Mic. 4:1–3):

---

12 Rightly, G. K. Beale, *The Temple and the Church's Mission: A Biblical Theology of the Dwelling Place of God*, NSBT 17 (Downers Grove, IL: InterVarsity Press, 2004), 335–64. Contra Jon D. Levenson, *Theology of the Program of Restoration of Ezekiel 40–48*, HSM 10 (Missoula, MT: Scholars Press, 1976), 45–46.

13 Daniel I. Block, *The Book of Ezekiel: Chapters 1–24*, NICOT (Grand Rapids, MI: Eerdmans, 1997), 59. See also Block, *Ezekiel 25–48*, 505–6, 510–11.

14 Thomas Renz, "The Use of the Zion Tradition in the Book of Ezekiel," in *Zion, City of Our God*, ed. Richard S. Hess and Gordon J. Wenham (Grand Rapids, MI: Eerdmans, 1999), 91.

15 William J. Dumbrell, *The Faith of Israel: A Theological Survey of the Old Testament*, 2nd ed. (Grand Rapids, MI: Baker Academic, 2002), 167.

16 Kalinda Rose Stevenson, *The Vision of Transformation: The Territorial Rhetoric of Ezekiel 40–48*, SBLDS 154 (Atlanta: Scholars Press, 1996), 5, 21, 23, 28, 35.

It shall come to pass in the latter days
    that the mountain of the house of the LORD
shall be established as the highest of the mountains,
    and it shall be lifted up above the hills;
and peoples shall flow to it,
    and many nations shall come, and say:
"Come, let us go up to the mountain of the LORD,
    to the house of the God of Jacob,
that he may teach us his ways
    and that we may walk in his paths."
For out of Zion shall go forth the law,
    and the word of the LORD from Jerusalem.
He shall judge between many peoples,
    and shall decide disputes for strong nations far away;
and they shall beat their swords into plowshares,
    and their spears into pruning hooks;
nation shall not lift up sword against nation,
    neither shall they learn war anymore.

Some think this passage refers to the millennium since there are still disputes among nations and there won't be such disputes in the new creation, but it is just as likely that Isaiah uses the language of his day to describe peace and salvation. In other words, this is a colorful way of saying that there will be universal peace forever. If we insist on taking the text literally, it doesn't apply to the millennium either, for we are told that "nation shall not lift up sword against nation / neither shall they learn war anymore" (Isa. 2:4), but such a statement doesn't fit with the millennium since the one thousand years conclude with a great war against the people of God (Rev. 20:7–10). The vision of peace found here is fulfilled in the new creation.

Third, one of the most famous texts that allegedly refer to the millennium is Isaiah 60. Zion's light has arrived, her sons and daughters will return, and nations will come to Zion bearing gifts. Table 7.2 shows how Revelation picks up language from Isaiah 60.

Table 7.2   Isaiah 60 and Revelation Compared

Isaiah 60		Revelation	
60:1–2	Light and glory on Zion	21:11	The city arrayed with God's glory
60:3–5, 11	Wealth of nations comes to Israel	21:24, 26	Kings bring their glory to the city
60:11	Gates always open	21:25	Gates will never close
60:14	Gentiles will bow before believing Jews	3:9	Unbelieving Jews will bow before believing Gentiles
60:16	Drinking the milk of the nations	21:24, 26	Glory of the nations brought into the city
60:19	God will be your glory	21:11	The city arrayed with God's glory
60:19–20	No sun, since God will be your light	21:23; 22:5	God and the Lamb are the city's light, so no need for sun and moon; no night there

In one other place, the New Testament alludes to Isaiah 60: 2 Peter 3:13 describes how righteousness dwells in the new heavens and new earth, echoing Isaiah 60:21, which proclaims that God's people will be righteous. What is striking is that every allusion to Isaiah 60 in the New Testament refers to the new creation, and not a single one refers to the millennium. Some say that the notion of bringing gifts to Zion in Isaiah could be a reality only in the millennium (Isa. 60:5, 11, 16), yet this text is cited not in Revelation 20 but in a text that speaks of the new creation (Rev. 21:24, 26). Therefore, we should not understand Isaiah 60 to be fulfilled literally, as if the nations actually bring gifts into the new Jerusalem. John is telling us that everything that is beautiful and lovely in the present creation will be in the world to come, but it will be present in a transmuted and elevated form.

Fourth, many premillennialists also point to Isaiah 65:17–25, which speaks of the new creation, and yet it also refers to those who die at one hundred, affirming that a person who dies before reaching one hundred will be considered cursed (Isa. 65:20). G. K. Beale has defended in a detailed article an amillennial reading of this text, though I don't follow him at every point.[17] I will sketch in a few arguments briefly. First, the text speaks directly of "new heavens and a new earth" (Isa. 65:17), and thus it is most natural to see this text as referring to the new creation rather than the millennium. Second, the coming of the new creation is aligned with a joyous future for Jerusalem (Isa. 65:18–19), and in Revelation 21:1–2 and 10, a new Jerusalem dawns with the new creation. Third, Isaiah says that "no more shall be heard in it the sound of weeping / and the cry of distress" (Isa. 65:19), and the day of no tears, as Revelation 21:1–4 specifically says, is when the new creation and new Jerusalem arrive. Fourth, the references to death in Isaiah 65:20 should be interpreted in light of the previous verse, which says that there will be no mourning or crying. If friends and loved ones are truly dying, there would still be intense grief, no matter how old one is. I suggest, then, that we have another example of what we saw in Ezekiel 40–48. The notions that no infants die and that people live to be one hundred, symbolizing fullness of years, are tokens of paradise. The references to death, then, should not be taken literally. To say that no one dies before one hundred is akin to living in Eden, but the text doesn't literally mean people die, since there is no mourning. Fifth, we see in Isaiah 65:25 that the curses of the old creation have ended, and thus "the wolf and the lamb shall graze together; / the lion shall eat straw like the ox." The promise of Genesis 3:15, where the offspring of the woman will crush the serpent, is completely fulfilled because the serpent will eat dust, which symbolizes total defeat. Isaiah 65:25 is clear; no evil will be done any longer on the Lord's "holy mountain," but if sin and death still exist, then evil continues. Since the curse of the old creation is overcome, it is difficult to see how we should interpret Isaiah 65:20 as envisioning the continuance of death because in

---

17   G. K. Beale, "An Amillennial Response to a Premillennial View of Isaiah 65:20," *JETS* 61, no. 3 (2018): 461–92.

Genesis 2–3, death is the fundamental manifestation of the curse. And the cessation of the curse means that death is conquered forever. Once again, we need to realize that the Old Testament prophets describe the future in the idiom and language of their day, and also, as Beale shows clearly, there are a number of indications in Isaiah 65:17–25 itself that we should not interpret death there literally.

Many think the binding of Satan decisively counters an amillennial interpretation. Satan is cast to the *earth* in Revelation 12:9 but is confined to the *abyss* and thus banned from the earth in 20:1–3. Satan deceives the world while on earth, but in chapter 20, the world is deceived only after the dragon is released from prison. While he is in the abyss, the nations are not deceived. The argument is a good one, but it isn't decisive.[18] The reference to the abyss in chapter 20 should not be construed to say that Satan isn't active on earth. The language is metaphorical, just as Hades and Death are metaphors in 6:7–8. When we read the text carefully, we see that the binding of Satan is delimited; he is bound "so that he might not deceive the nations any longer" (20:3). In the Old Testament, the nations were deceived and outside the citizenship of Israel and cut off from God and the Messiah (Eph. 2:11–13). Israel was God's special people, and the nations were opposed to God's purposes. Now the deception of the nations is removed so that some from every tribe, tongue, people, and nation believe (Rev. 5:9). Satan still blinds the minds of unbelievers (2 Cor. 4:4), and the entire world remains under his power (1 John 5:19). But his ability to deceive *entire nations* has been removed, and the whole world is being blessed in fulfillment of the promise to Abraham (Gen. 12:3). Satan has been bound at the cross (Matt. 12:29), and he has been cast out as Jesus has been lifted up and glorified on the cross (John 12:31). The two pictures of Satan in Revelation 12 and 20, then, are complementary. Yes, he still deceives human beings, but he is no longer able to deceive the entirety of the Gentile world. And because of the work of Jesus Christ on the

---

18 Cf. G. K. Beale, *The Book of Revelation: A Commentary on the Greek Text*, NIGTC (Grand Rapids, MI: Eerdmans, 1999), 984–95.

cross, he has no grounds for accusing the saints. The binding of Satan will be lifted near the end of history when the man of lawlessness enters the scene and the mystery of lawlessness bursts into full flower (2 Thess. 2:4–12), and then we will see a remarkable intensification of evil before the end arrives.

The best argument for the premillennial reading rests on premillennialists' understanding of the resurrection in Revelation 20, especially when we consider that amillennialists claim that the first resurrection is spiritual and that the resurrection of the rest (i.e., unbelievers) is physical. Still, the amillennial interpretation is also plausible. We see from Romans 6:4–13 and John 5:24–29 that the language of spiritual and physical resurrection are used together in the same context, and thus the idea that resurrection in Revelation 20 must refer to the physical resurrection is questionable. Meredith Kline's reading of the text is fascinating and perhaps the best defense for amillennialism.[19] Table 7.3 captures Kline's understanding of Revelation 20:1–6.

Table 7.3   Meredith Kline's Reading of Revelation 20:1–6

First death	Physical death of the saints	*First resurrection*	Spiritual resurrection of the saints
Second death	Spiritual death of the wicked	*Second resurrection*	Physical resurrection of the saints

Revelation 20:1–6 mentions only the first resurrection and the second death, but Kline points out that "first" in Scripture often refers to the preconsummated state. Thus, there is a first Adam and a second Adam (Rom. 5:12–19; 1 Cor. 15:21–22, 45–46), a first covenant and a new covenant (cf. Luke 22:20; 1 Cor. 11:25; 2 Cor. 3:6; Gal. 3:17; Heb. 8:6–13; 9:1, 15, 18; 12:24). So too in Revelation, the first resurrection is spiritual and preliminary to the second resurrection, which is physical and eternal. In a similar way, physical death is, for the wicked, a prelude

19 Meredith G. Kline, "The First Resurrection," *WTJ* 37, no. 3 (1975): 366–75.

of the second death, of eternal death. The word "resurrection" typically refers to physical resurrection, but it isn't surprising to find that the word is used symbolically in an apocalyptic book. The first resurrection refers to the intermediate state, to the life believers receive when they die in the Lord (2 Cor. 5:6, 8; Phil. 1:21–23). John speaks of the "souls of those who had been beheaded" in Revelation 20:4, and thus it makes sense to see souls coming to life as referring to the intermediate state. We also see a reference to "souls" who are martyred in 6:9–11, and yet they are praying to the Lord for justice, which strengthens the case for a spiritual resurrection. The reigning for one thousand years in an amillennial reading is symbolic, and hence it isn't significant whether they reign for the entire period. The point is that martyred believers triumph.

Conclusion

Is the amillennial interpretation convincing? It has many strengths since it fits with the reading of the entirety of the Scriptures, but the premillennial position in many ways seems to be a more natural way to explain Revelation 20. Fortunately, one's judgment on this matter isn't critical for the faith, and many believers assign too much significance to the millennial question. It isn't a weakness to admit that certainty is hard to come by, and there are solid reasons for saying that there are good arguments for both positions. We need to remember, whatever our position on the millennium, that it doesn't last forever but that the new creation is eternal, where we see our God face-to-face.

Epilogue

IN A WORLD FULL OF EVIL, selfishness, materialism, and sexual exploitation, John proclaims a message of hope, although it is an apocalyptic message that is hidden from the world. Thus believers must attune their ears to hear a transcendent message, to hear the words of the Son of Man and the Holy Spirit. Unbelievers stop their ears and refuse to listen and become deaf to what God says. We are told that evil will not finally triumph, even if it now seems that it is unconquerable. We find in Revelation a parody of the Trinity, for the forces of evil center on the dragon, the beast, and the false prophet. At the same time, evil finds its home in the city of man instead of the city of God, in the harlot Babylon instead of the heavenly Jerusalem. Despite the power and lure of evil, goodness will finally triumph, the world will be renewed, and all that is wicked will be removed.

John writes to encourage the saints to hear and heed, to listen and obey, to pay attention and persevere. The forces of evil beckon believers, summoning them to compromise and to join hands with those opposed to God. John reminds believers of the great reward that awaits them if they remain faithful, if they refuse to throw in their lot with the beast and Babylon, with the ancient serpent and the evil religious system propagated by the second beast. Everlasting joy belongs to those who overcome and conquer, to those who continue to walk in God's ways.

What believers need is a vision of God and of Christ. John reminds readers of God's sovereignty and lordship. They do not serve an ineffectual and weak Lord, for he is the Creator of all things, and thus he has the power to judge and to save. Nothing in the universe takes place apart from his will. The suffering they endure, as difficult as it may be, is under his rule and authority. The demonic powers of evil may think they are steering the world in a certain direction, but God remains at the helm and is working out his good purposes.

The key to history is hidden from the world (which is why believers must hear the message from the Spirit), but it lies in the death and resurrection of the Lamb of God. The Lord does not first conquer evil in the world by wiping out and destroying evil, although that day will come. The Lord wins the victory over Satan through sacrificial love, by means of the death of his Son. Suffering love is the path to victory, showing that love is stronger than hate and that, in the end, love wins. This should not be read to say that there will be no final judgment. Indeed, Revelation emphasizes that judgment is certainly coming, but God gives the world an opportunity for repentance and salvation. Judgment comes on those who have rejected the suffering love of God in the death of Christ. The Holy Spirit points readers to the great act of Christ's redeeming love, and this same love triumphs over the devil and casts him out of heaven—and thus Satan no longer has any basis for accusing the saints. The Spirit bears witness to Jesus Christ as the Lamb of God, as the one who spilled his blood so that the clothing of believers is white and clean.

Revelation opens a window into the world to come, reminding us that there is a new world coming, that a new creation is dawning, and that all that is evil and wicked will pass away. Some think there will be a millennium on earth first; others think the millennial age is a present reality. Whatever one makes of the millennium, it is a temporary period. The millennium is not of ultimate importance since it doesn't last forever. What matters more is the world without end that is coming. In that world there are no tears, no pain, and no death. The agony of the old creation has passed away, and the joy of dwelling with God and the Lamb will never grow old. The entire world will be a new temple, a new

Jerusalem, the dwelling place of God. It will be a place of perfect safety and unrivaled beauty, of serene peace and unending joy. John writes so that the readers will continue to believe and persevere because he wants them to enjoy that world, and he wants us to enjoy it too. And thus we should hear and heed what he says.

General Index

abyss, 34, 90, 96, 165, 176
Adam, 177
adultery, 56
adversary, 42–43
age to come, 52
"all the tribes of the earth," 135, 136
Almighty, 71
Alpha and Omega, 71, 107
amillennialism, 163, 166, 168–78
Ancient of Days, 121
angel
    commands John to worship God
      alone, 110
    communicates revelation to John,
      26
    as fellow servant, 75
angelic measurements, 152
angel of the Lord, 137
angels, 28, 106, 144–46
annihilation, 100
Antiochus II, 58
Antiochus IV Epiphanes, 43, 130
Antipas, 56
apocalyptic revelation, 24–29
    and amillennial interpretation, 168
    book of Revelation as, 22
    fluidity of, 147
    purposes of, 26
    reveals true state of affairs, 31, 34
    symbolizes end of history, 81
Apollyon, 90
Arianism, 107
Armageddon, 50, 96, 170

Athanasius, 120
atonement, 118
Augustus, Emperor, 56
Aune, David, 24, 25, 113, 145

Babylon, 34, 44, 179
    glorified itself, 40, 97
    glory of, 158
    the harlot, 39–40
    judgment of, 51, 94, 96–98
    as mystery, 97
    as wicked whore, 143
Bauckham, Richard, 22, 28, 35, 40,
    63, 73, 82–88, 107, 108–9, 129,
    145n6
Beale, G. K., 31–32, 38n13, 62, 68, 84,
    86, 97, 111, 117n26, 150, 175–76
beast, 34–38, 44
    human, not divine, 37
    worship of, 33
    wound of, 35
beauty of the Lord, 73
beginning and the end, 107
believers
    must conquer, 131–32
    receiving a crown, 133
    vindication at second coming, 136
Bignon, Guillaume, 72
black horse, 79
blamelessness, 127
blessedness, 149, 158
    eschatological dimension of, 49–53
"blessed" sayings, 47–53

I AM WHO I AM, 70
idolatry, 32, 41, 56, 92, 97, 127
"I know," 105
imperial authority, 62
imperial cult, 38, 42, 56
incense and prayers of the saints, 82
inheritance, 60
"in the Spirit," 142–43
interadvent period, 79, 80
intermediate state, 178
Irenaeus, 19–20, 21, 162
iron rod, 131
Isaiah, 25, 138
Israel
    harlotry of, 32–33, 40
    return from exile, 133
    spiritual meaning, 123
"it was given," 68–69

Jerome, 21
Jerusalem, destruction of (AD 70), 76,
    77, 88, 133
Jesus Christ
    atoning work of, 115–19, 132
    blood of, 130
    as both Lion and Lamb, 116
    as center of Revelation, 99, 103
    deity of, 104–13
    eschatological discourse of, 76–77
    eyes "like a flame of fire," 105, 137
    as "Faithful and True," 137
    as a faithful witness, 115
    fully divine and fully human, 120
    judgment of, 135–39
    lordship of, 112
    as Messiah, 132, 139
    return of, 132–35, 136
        amillennialism on, 168
        postmillennialism on, 163
    rides a white horse, 105, 137
    rule over all creation, 107
    rules over nations with iron rod,
        130–31
    sacrifice of, 129
    shares same identity as God, 139
    sovereignty of, 104

suffering and death of, 132
sword in mouth, 138, 163
victory over Satan, 132, 180
voice like the roar of many waters,
    105–6
will come like a thief, 50, 58
worship of, 111
worthy to open the scroll, 116–17, 120
Jews, persecuting Christians, 123
Jezebel, 58
John, emphasis on divine authority in
    his writings, 23
judgment, 67, 75–103, 138
    of Babylon, 51, 94, 96–99
    emphasis in Revelation, 100–101
    justice of, 94–95
    as true and just, 99
    of unbelievers, 91
justice, 100–101
Justin Martyr, 162, 164

keeping the words of Revelation, 49
kingdom of priests, 104
King of kings, 110
King of the nations, 71–72
Kline, Meredith G., 177
knowing someone's name, 137
Koester, Craig, 36–37, 42n18, 56n6,
    100n18, 133n49

Ladd, George, 28
lake of fire, 55, 137, 169
Lamb of God, 116, 117
    death and resurrection of, 180
    and salvation, 113–22
    shared identity with God, 108–11
    as worthy, 108
lampstands, 62
Laodicea, 51, 59
Leviathan, 42
light and glory of God, will shine on
    his people, 155
linguistic level (interpretation of
    Revelation), 27
Lion of the tribe of Judah, 112, 116
locusts, 90

"who was and is and is to come,"
     70–71, 94
wicked, judgment at second coming,
     136
wine of God's wrath, 99
winepress, 114, 138
woman
     flees to the wilderness, 43, 131
     preserved in the wilderness, 134
     suffers anguish of childbirth, 130

"Word of God," 111–12
"word of their testimony," 60
worship of God, 52, 74–75, 92–93
wrath of God, 95, 99, 100, 109, 122
wrath of the Lamb, 109, 122
Wright, N. T., 166

Zechariah, 135–36
     apocalyptic in, 25
     vision of, 77–78

Scripture Index

Also Available in the
New Testament Theology Series

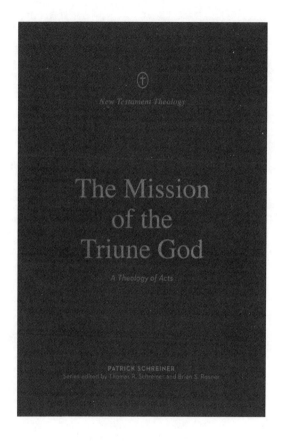

New Testament Theology

The Mission
of the
Triune God

A Theology of Acts

PATRICK SCHREINER
Series edited by Thomas R. Schreiner and Brian S. Rosner

For more information, visit **crossway.org**.